# One Half Crown from Hoboken

# One Half Crown from Hoboken

*a memoir*

Jim Ray

The stories in this book reflect the author's recollection of events. Some names, locations, and identifying characteristics have been changed to protect the privacy of those depicted. Dialog has been reconstructed to the best of the author's memory.

Copyright © 2022 by Jim Ray
All rights reserved. Published in the United States by Orchard Knob Group LLC.

www.orchardknob.com

Library of Congress Control Number: 2022939573

ISBN 979-8-9853696-0-1 (hardcover)
ISBN 979-8-9853696-1-8 (ebook)

Jacket design by Melanie Pernell Ray
Jacket description and author bio by Adam Colwell

Printed in the United States of America
First edition: June 2022

*For Stacey*

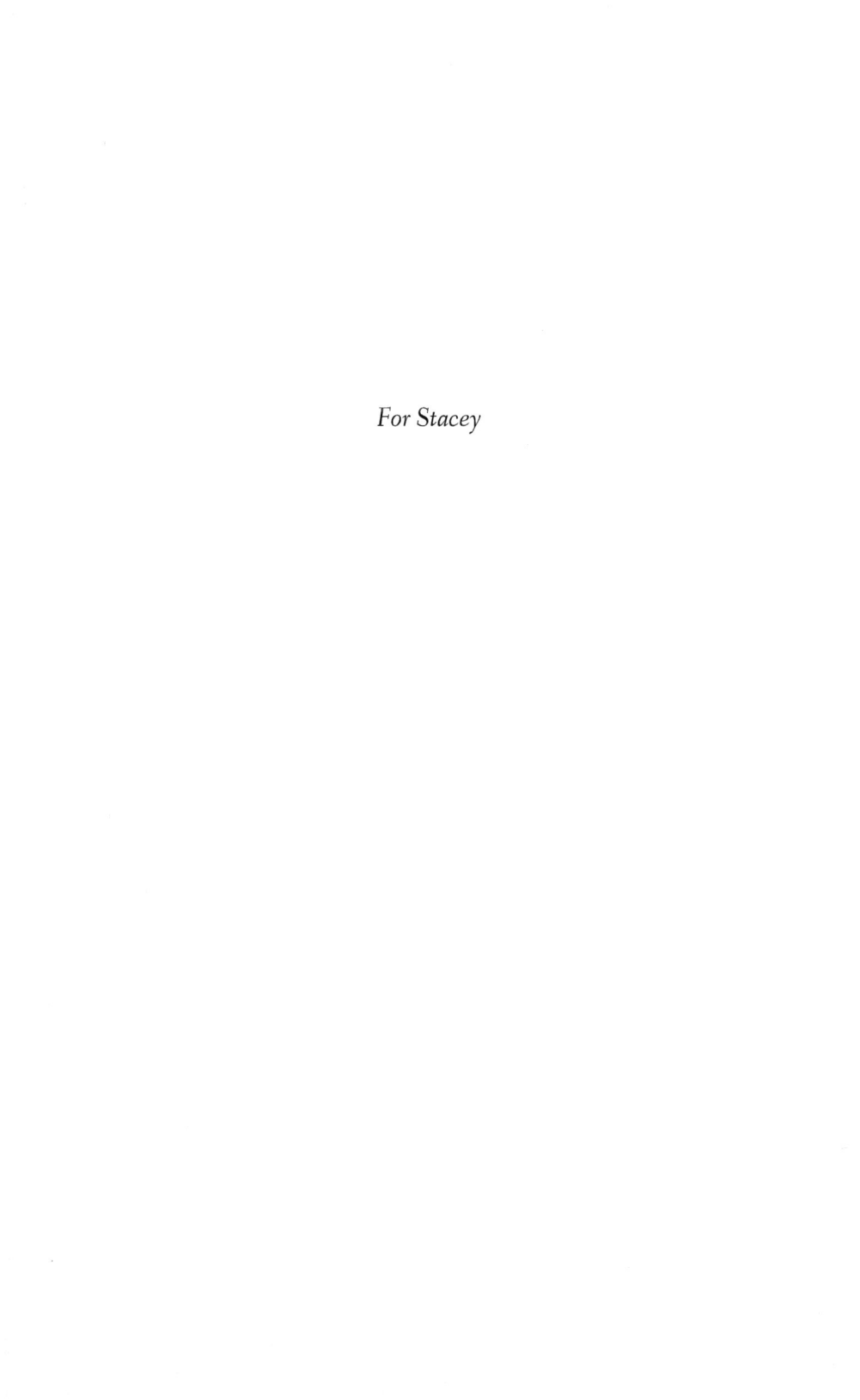

# Contents

1. The Doctor — 1
2. The Barrels — 5
3. Esj — 9
4. Wonderfully Made — 16
5. The Oatmeal (Part One) — 22
6. The Oatmeal (Part Two) — 31
7. Football — 38
8. Applying One's Self — 47
9. Piano Lessons — 53
10. A Stoppage of Joy — 60
11. The Meow Machine — 66
12. The Kingswood Senior Centre — 73
13. The Kiss — 85
14. The Larramore Scratch — 92
15. Any Yard for $12.95 — 101
16. Getting Right with Brother Melvin — 107
17. Frank Woodfin and the Big Red Truck — 119
18. We Know Who You Are — 129
19. The Whoppers — 138
20. The Church of Your Choice — 143
21. The Polar Bear Club — 153
22. The Pickle Contest — 164
23. Jesus and the Timberlands — 172
24. The Great Buggy Repossession — 180
25. The TV Dinner — 192
26. Trying — 198
27. The Cat — 201
28. Amwaylaid — 209
29. The Deal — 216
30. The Miser — 222
31. The Pastor — 227

| | |
|---|---|
| 32. The Church Lady | 231 |
| 33. The Call | 235 |
| 34. The Question | 237 |
| 35. The Midnight Run | 244 |
| 36. The Inheritance | 251 |
| 37. The First Rule | 256 |
| 38. The Derby | 262 |

# One Half Crown from Hoboken

# Chapter 1

## *The Doctor*

You can tolerate a bit of hubris in your doctor if he's really good, and this guy was supposed to be the best.

In case anyone had any doubt, there were pictures of babies all over the place.

Not average babies, mind you, because your average baby is ugly, I think.

But beautiful, perfect babies. And toddlers and preteens and adolescents too, all smiling and happy and well-nourished. The infants were positively cherubic, every one of them. The children with their white teeth and wavy hair and blue eyes. And not a pimple to be found anywhere on the teenagers, unblemished in their crisp baseball uniforms and cheerleader outfits.

Pictures of success.

They all owed their very existence to the Doctor. They came to be because of him. Who could blame him for being cocksure? You would be too if your mailbox spilled over every day with glamour shots of all these little wonders you had created, supplemented by gushing letters of praise from the parents who were only parents because of you.

---

THE DOOR OPENED and the Doctor came into the room. He was trim and fit and tan. The hairline was receding some now, but even that seemed not so much a deficiency as an accentuation of his soaring intellect. This time he was limping, though, letting out a little groan with each step.

Slowly he sank into his wingback and hoisted a leg gingerly onto the coffee table. Groaned again.

It was obvious he wanted us to inquire.

I did not really care but felt obliged.

What happened to your leg? I asked.

This query provided the green light the Doctor wanted, and it propelled him into a lengthy account of his recent bicycle accident, augmented with commentary on his penchant for speed and risk. How he loved adventure. Pushing the envelope. Caution to the wind.

He was so enchanted with himself that for several interminable minutes he seemed to have completely forgotten why we were there. It was important, it seemed, that we be apprised of his athletic prowess and daring. He was so much more than just a brilliant and beloved specialist.

My wife heard none of this. She was utterly fixated on the manila folder in his hand which, finally, he opened to address the matter in issue.

We had thousands of dollars and a mountain of prayer invested in whatever was in that folder. I was pretty sure it was going to be good news. The babies on the wall all but promised me it would be.

Plus, the alternative was unthinkable.

Literally.

I had never contemplated for a moment what we would do if we didn't get a positive outcome. Surely the God who loved us would not allow anything so harsh. And the Doctor had hardly been bashful about predicting ultimate triumph. Brimming with confidence from day one, he radiated poise that never diminished in the slightest through several fruitless procedures. Those, he didn't consider setbacks but simply—what was it he called it?—*part of the process*. And besides all that, there were the beautiful, smiling babies everywhere.

The Doctor looked down at the folder, scratched briefly at his temple, and puffed out his cheeks.

Well, it didn't work, he said flatly, we didn't get anything.

A few seconds elapsed as those words were processed. Or it may have been more than a few seconds. It's difficult to gauge time when you're being tased.

Eventually, my wife composed herself enough to ask the follow up: What does this mean?

It means you're done, he replied.

What a clumsy and incongruous response, I thought. Cruel, even. This was, after all, the man who'd been regaling us for months with dizzying explanations of high-tech drugs and innovative procedures and promising probabilities. Perhaps he had never actually used the word *guarantee*, but he'd most certainly never mentioned the possibility of failure. There were the references to journal articles he'd authored, and the annual picnic for all his patients and their swarms of children, and how lucky we were to be right here in Phoenix, Arizona with access to the best specialists in the world.

Him, in other words.

And there was the diploma from Johns Hopkins and a raft of professional commendations staring down at us from every wall. Not to mention, also, the pictures of the babies.

I was expecting something more, maybe something with a little medical terminology. Maybe something with a touch of compassion. Something with a vein of hope running through it, however thin.

Didn't get any of that.

You're done.

That's all he had for us. It was direct and unambiguous. I'll give him that.

---

THE DESPAIR WAS ALREADY STARTING to press down on my chest when we stood to leave, but I knew whatever I was feeling was nothing compared to what my wife was feeling. She was the one who had been taking the brunt of it. The shots, and the drugs in triple doses, and the endless prodding. She was the one who had been dealing with friends and relatives and the daily questions that were well-meaning but stabbing.

She was the one who had cried every night since I don't know when.

*You're done.*

The words were on a loop now, playing over in my head.

Everything was a fog, except that when we reached the parking lot I had the presence to slip into the driver's seat of Stacey's car, a 1989 V6 Chevrolet Beretta GT. She drives fast as a rule, notably faster when she's upset. The speed increases exponentially in correlation with her level of distress. Even though we were done, I didn't really want to die.

That would come later.

# Chapter 2

## *The Barrels*

Most kids eagerly awaited a visit from Santa Claus. We dreamed about the day the barrels would arrive.

The barrels were better.

My dad decided from the get-go he wasn't going to foist the Santa prevarication on us, and so my sister and I never believed in him, ever.

I am not going to lie to you, Dad would say, there is no such thing as Santa Claus. You can thank me and your mom for the presents. That fat guy in the red polyester standing out in front of Revco has nothing to do with it.

Some people—relatives especially—thought this to be cruel. A deprivation of the wonder of childhood, they said, vigorously admonishing Dad for stealing away the magic of Christmas.

He was unmoved.

Lie to your kids if you want to, he said, but I'm not lying to mine.

I always thought it was a good decision. Knowledge is power, and the mere fact that I alone knew my friends had pinned their hopes and dreams to a silly myth was, honestly, an enjoyable position from which to operate. I was instructed to keep the information to myself but on occasion—like when a debate arose on the playground about who was stupider—I found it useful and devastatingly effective to reveal the truth.

There were other benefits. I never suffered the trauma of discovering Santa wasn't real. Never was troubled by the perception that my parents didn't get me anything for Christmas. And—unencumbered by the ludicrous notion of my presents sitting up there at the North Pole until Christmas Eve—I frequently searched for and found them before December twenty five.

Anyway, Santa would have been a feeble sideshow because the best day was not Christmas but the arrival of the barrels.

---

MY DAD WAS A MISSIONARY. Shipping your belongings was tricky back then. From somewhere he found these big metal drums—twenty of them, about—at a discount. He had them steam cleaned and used them to transfer our stuff all over the world. After every move, we kept the barrels because we knew we would be moving again soon enough.

The first big move I remember was to Australia. The only thing was, we traveled by plane while the barrels came by ship.

It took them a long time to get there.

A really long time.

It took them so long, in fact, we mostly forgot what was in them. By the time the barrels arrived, it was like getting all new stuff.

I'll grant you the waiting period was excruciating. We lived for ages on whatever we had managed to wedge into a few suitcases, and there was no room for nonessentials, as defined by the adults.

And it was difficult to explain the predicament to new friends, given that the warmth of your welcome to the neighborhood was dependent in large part on the quality of the toys you brought with you. We started with nothing.

Why don't you have any toys? They asked.

We do, but they are in the barrels.

What barrels?

The ones coming from America.

When will the barrels get here?

We don't know. Soon. Tomorrow, maybe. Or the next day.

Of course it wasn't tomorrow or the next day or anything of the sort, but hope never dies, not if your barrels are out there floating around somewhere in the Pacific Ocean.

Every day we waited in anguish, desperate to see the truck trundling up the street bearing the barrels. Every night I brought the same requests before God. I prayed for my family. I prayed for my grandmother in America. Most fervently of all I prayed for the barrels.

Jesus, please make the barrels come tomorrow.

I sat on the front steps, on the curb, on the fence, hour after hour, day after day.

Where are the barrels? Dear God, when will they ever get here?

Inside, too, every moment was heavy with longing for the barrels. I listened intently for the sound of a straining diesel, wishing each faint rumble would be the one to deliver the toys.

―――

AND THEN ONE DAY, almost miraculously, they arrived, the neighborhood kids collecting on the sidewalk in awe as two greasy men wrestled them off the flatbed and into the driveway. No one had ever witnessed such a spectacle.

Each barrel was sealed airtight with a heavy-duty metal collar and clamp. You needed brute force to open them, and Dad was the only one strong enough to do it. It was sheer guesswork as to what might be in which barrel, but there was frenzied lobbying nonetheless conducted by my sister and me.

Open this barrel.

No, please open this one first.

There's just books in this one, Dad. Try that one.

No, don't listen to her. Open this one next.

I think my stuff is in this one.

This is it... these are my toys!

I forgot I had this!

I would play with my rediscovered treasures for a while and then return for more wonderment as additional barrels were opened. There was my plastic lawnmower and Rock 'Em Sock 'Em Robots and Crashmobile and Legos and GI Joes and Matchbox cars and pop guns and the Viewmaster. It went on for ages. It was like every Christmas and birthday of your life compressed into a few hours of unmitigated excitement.

And the neighborhood kids—the ones who had begun to doubt and scoff at this outlandish tale of barrels allegedly filled with American toys that would be here someday—were stupefied by the sight of it.

Jubilation. Relief. Exhilaration. Fun. Answered prayers. Endless entertainment. Instant popularity. It all came in the barrels.

Santa?

Please.

# Chapter 3
## *Esj*

I used to worry a lot about being adopted.

I was not actually adopted, as far as I can tell, but my sister ESJ promulgated this notion so aggressively for so long that I still have the odd doubt.

ESJ is not my sister's official name. Her name is really Joy, but I call her ESJ, which stands for Evil Sister Joy. You will see why here in a minute.

This all started one night as I was curled in bed trying to go to sleep when ESJ called to me from her bedroom across the hall.

I'm not supposed to tell you this, she said. Mom and Dad told me not to say anything, but you're adopted. Your real parents didn't like you. We don't either, but we're stuck with you.

You're lying, I replied hesitantly.

When you are five years old it's hard to know when you are being deceived.

I'm not lying, she countered. I wouldn't lie about something like that. I just wanted you to know the truth.

By the time my feet hit the floor, the tears were welling up. I galloped down the hall and into the kitchen. Mom saw the trauma on my face and thought, at best, the house was on fire. What on earth is the matter? she asked.

Am I adopted? I blurted out, by now sobbing and completely unhinged.

You're not adopted, said my dad.

Of course you're not adopted, added Mom. Where did you get that idea?

From Joy.

ESJ was summoned into the kitchen and admonished for telling lies. Clearly, though, she felt the impact had been well worth the consequences, as evidenced by the fact that she would go on to repeat this allegation several thousand more times in ensuing years.

---

ON THE WHOLE, my sister has evolved into a relatively nice adult person. She calls often now to tell me she loves me. I appreciate the Christmas presents and birthday greetings and gift cards. But it's hard to forget what it was like for me when she was full of malice. Her singular purpose in life, prior to reaching the age of maturity and leaving home, was to keep me bracketed in a constant state of terror and misery. At that she was enormously successful.

There is a story, retold at family gatherings with great mirth, about how when I arrived home from the hospital after my birth she immediately poured a glass of cold water on my head, just to see what I would do.

I don't have a personal recollection of that, but I do remember the first time I was allowed out of the house as a toddler to play on my own. ESJ instructed me to sit in a puddle.

When I didn't respond to the directive with sufficient haste, she supplied a helpful push. And then she promptly reported to Mom that I was playing in the mud.

Anything I did was immediately conveyed, usually with considerable embellishment, to my parents. Many stories were manufactured out of whole cloth. For some reason, she was always deemed the more credible party in cases of conflicting testimony.

I was not allowed to hit girls. If you hit your sister, my parents said, you would hit your wife someday. So don't you ever hit a girl, especially your sister. People who hit their sisters end up in jail when they grow up, they told me.

But this injunction only traveled in one direction, and it had the effect of rendering me a veritable punching bag. After receiving twenty or thirty blows I would strike back timidly in desperation, and then at once be reported and punished.

Jim hit me! Jim hit me! she would wail, implying she had been gratuitously attacked while minding her own business.

Why did you hit her? Dad would ask, not waiting for an answer as he unfastened his belt. You know better than to ever, ever hit a girl.

But she hit me first, I argued. Like a hundred times!

It doesn't matter. I told you to never hit a girl. And the leather would come flying.

---

IN ADDITION to arranging matters so I would be constantly in trouble with the parents, ESJ also insinuated my punishment would continue into the afterlife.

You're going to hell, she informed me one day.

Why?

Because you have not asked Jesus into your heart.

To prove this wasn't just speculation, she showed me some frightening Bible passages supporting her analysis. And so I asked Jesus into my heart. That closed the matter of my eternal security for a few weeks, but then ESJ felt it needed to be revisited.

You might still be going to hell, she said.

No, I'm not. I asked Jesus into my heart.

But you probably didn't really mean it, came the rebuttal. And God knows if you didn't really mean it. If you didn't mean it, it doesn't count.

Thanks to ESJ and her doubt-mongering, I asked Jesus into my heart almost every night for about a decade.

———

THERE WAS, I later learned, an official procedure for dispensing with such doubts in the Baptist church. Something they called *seeking assurance of salvation*.

When they gave the altar call after the sermon, there were five things you could go up for. Some churches even had response cards with the five options and checkboxes already printed. The first option was salvation. The second was baptism. The third was church membership. The fourth was rededication. And the fifth option was called assurance of salvation. If you went forward during the altar call, it had to be for one of those five things.

If you went up seeking assurance of salvation, it meant you had previously claimed to have been saved but now you weren't sure if the decision had really taken hold—so now you were doing it again just to be on the safe side.

At the end of the altar call one of the deacons would pass the response cards to the pastor and he would read all the names and announce what they had come up for. So and so has come forward for assurance of salvation, he would say, and there would be a smattering of amens and praise the Lords from the congregation.

People didn't get as excited about an assurance of salvation decision as they did for a straight salvation or baptism.

I normally went through my assurance of salvation rituals in the privacy of my bedroom at night. Going forward in church was extremely humiliating and attached suspicions to you that were very hard to shake off. There were those who went forward for assurance of salvation almost every week, and they were assumed to be either deranged or trying to atone for some habitual, embarrassingly heinous sins.

There was this one occasion, though, when our church showed a movie called *The Burning Hell*. It was so horrifying, every single person in the building surged forward on the altar call to get saved or receive assurance of salvation, or both.

*The Burning Hell* was filmed by a preacher from Mississippi named Estus Pirkle—that was his real name, apparently—who somehow got his hands on some movie cameras and a lot of fake blood and other ghoulish paraphernalia from a Hollywood back lot garage sale. He then rounded up a regiment of profoundly amateurish actors.

The story, which reappeared to me in many subsequent nightmares, centered around two hippies who came to visit Brother Pirkle. One of the hippies listened to the Reverend's message and repented, but the other one made fun of him and rejected his warnings about hell. Brother Pirkle cautioned the non-receptive hippie he was making a grave mistake, but he just laughed in the preacher's face, and told him there was no hell and even if there was, all his buddies would be there anyway. He then took off on his motorcycle. About a mile down the road there was a gruesome accident in which he was decapitated, and then went promptly to hell.

The movie showed the hippie arriving in hell where he was personally greeted by Satan, who was moderately obese and—judging by his accent—from Alabama.

In addition to the hippie story there was also a lot of screaming, and maggots crawling out of people's eyes, and at one point in the movie the earth opened up and a whole tribe of scoffers was swallowed up and dropped at high velocity into the abyss.

Such was the power of *The Burning Hell*, some viewers went forward twice on the same altar call, something never seen before or since.

Really.

They went forward and accepted Jesus for salvation, and then they went back to their seat, and as the invitation droned on through several dozen stanzas, they got to thinking about the maggots again, and the hippie's head rolling around on the ground and what not. And they went forward again for assurance of salvation. A lot of them got haircuts the next morning, too.

---

APART FROM SEEING *The Burning Hell*, though, I think I would have been fully confident in my salvation but for the endless meddling and spiritual mind games of ESJ.

Many other mean things were said on a regular basis to exacerbate my insecurities, including but not limited to—

You're ugly.

You will never, ever get a date. Ever.

You're skinny.

You smell.

Your nose is massive.

You're dumb.

You have a huge backside.

You will never get a job.

Your chest is like a pancake, but at least it matches your stick arms.

Etc, etc.

This is why I use the moniker ESJ instead of Joy. Someone with the name of Joy should be bringing you happiness, not making you worried every time the doorbell rings it's going to be someone from the orphanage arriving to repossess you.

## Chapter 4

## *Wonderfully Made*

I HAVE NOT ALWAYS, TO BE CANDID, BEEN EXCITED ABOUT going to church, even when they are not showing *The Burning Hell*. For one thing, churches seem to insist on scheduling services concurrently with important sporting events. And there are also a lot of preachers—the majority, maybe—who would be unable to meet the minimum excitement threshold required to appear as guests on C-span.

Yet the worst thing that can happen to you in church is not a boring preacher. The worst thing that can happen to you is to be recruited to work in the church nursery, that intense crucible of whining, screaming, saliva, mucus and effluvia.

Thankfully this did not happen to me much until I was an adult. No one in their right mind would ask a teenage boy to help in the nursery. Even most teenage girls are iffy, but teenage boys do not pay attention to anything and are liable to drop babies on their heads or allow them to ingest building blocks or—at the very least—not bother with changing a diaper until it explodes.

If the teenage girl is Stacey, however, that is a different matter altogether.

The only dream she ever had was to be a mom.

———

STACEY MAY HAVE BEEN the youngest ever paid staff member in the history of church nurserydom. Your babies were safe with Stacey. She took care of other people's babies better than they did.

Stacey was dreaming about babies when she was scarcely more than a baby herself. Certainly long before it was explained to her how the actual process of baby creation worked. She was commonly to be found running around the house with a pillow stuffed up her shirt, pretending to be an expectant preschooler.

Pregnancy was to her a total fascination. The whole concept of a baby growing inside someone's belly—an incredible, beautiful, miraculous thing. And all the minutiae that went along with it, like trimesters and back pain and placentas and breast feeding.

I did not meet Stacey until much later but would have surely found the whole thing to be ludicrous and unseemly.

Babies—and how they are created—were not anywhere on my list of interests during the formative years, although I was subjected to distasteful details about how the process worked, dutifully explained by my mom to ESJ and me.

ESJ enjoyed the sessions and requested they be repeated regularly, while I found every moment to be extraordinarily discomforting and tried my best to block out the memories of them.

———

MOM HAD this book called *Wonderfully Made*, written by some Lutheran lady in America. It had a lot of colorful drawings. They were innocuous enough in the early pages but quickly became disturbing as you progressed through the book.

It started out with drawings of a boy carrying a football and a girl jumping rope. Then it showed them growing up to be young people, and then eventually adults with their own baby. At this point the mother was holding a cooking pot with apron strings trailing behind her, and the man was donned in a spiffy blue suit carrying a briefcase. At all times they were brimming with happiness.

The book indicated that in the not-too-distant future I would find girls to be much more interesting. This seemed highly implausible. It also claimed I would soon notice changes to my body and noted assuringly that this was perfectly normal and OK. Along with this information was a picture of the man smiling as he lifted the girl off her horse. She was smiling as well. The horse appeared to be indifferent. I did not really know at first what the Lutheran lady meant about the body changes except that when it happened it would evidently cause a lot of smiling, and possibly equestrianism.

A few pages later things started to get really unpleasant. The man was now pictured standing next to an image of a giant sperm, and the woman was accompanied by what the book said was an egg, although it was more like a giant yellow bowling ball. This alone put me off boiled eggs for a good while.

Anyway, the couple looked very pleased to be in possession of these valuable reproductive items. Then there were drawings of their midsections along with revolting images of the scrotum, testicles, ovaries, vulva, uterus and Fallopian tubes.

Later, the book noted, I would probably hear boys in the washroom at school talk about body parts using words that were incorrect, but the book was going to teach me the proper terms.

The Lutheran lady was mostly right about the incorrect words although I do not ever recall hearing a washroom equivalent term for Fallopian tubes.

After enduring several sittings of reading *Wonderfully Made* I made it known I was ready to move on to other topics. I asked that it be put away and protested strongly whenever any attempt was made to take it off the shelf.

I did not know that many years later I would be back to listening about all the different body parts that go into making a baby and finding out it didn't always work out for everyone the way the book showed.

———

Nobody was smiling after the Doctor said we were done. We went home and had a good long cry, and I called my parents and told them they shouldn't be expecting to get any grandchildren from me. And the family tree would have to be extended through ESJ's genes, which was a fearful proposition.

The next day after I left glumly for work, Stacey shook off the trauma and began furtively calling every adoption agency in town. There was no particular concern on her part about whether the baby would be procured from China or Russia or some illicit third world country. The singular issue was that she wanted a baby and was going to have to get one from somewhere. It didn't seem to matter that we had discussed this plan not at all.

I arrived home in the afternoon and was immediately attacked with a blizzard of information about alternative methods of becoming an adoptive parent.

This is not the time for this, I said.

It's the perfect time for it, she replied.

No, it's not, I said with mounting frustration.

We were sitting in the kitchen and I briefly but quite seriously contemplated running my head through the window next to the table, in the hope the shattering glass would nick my jugular.

Look, I said, we've just been told less than twenty-four hours ago that we were done. We need some time to process this and consider our options. We can't just go berserk and start applying to random adoption agencies or trying to steal a baby from someone off the street. This is crazy.

You can't fix this, she said. You always think you can fix stuff. And you can't fix this. Not this time. I'm moving on to the next logical choice.

I looked down at her notes. She had telephone numbers and bullet points and arrows and names of countries and adoption agencies and all manner of graffiti. Here and there were block letters, a digit or two, several items circled or followed by an exclamation point.

I had no choice but to inject the irrefutable argument.

May I remind you of something? I asked. We don't have any money left.

There was a long silence. What little we had, we had paid to the Doctor.

The harsh reality recap sucked the life right out of her.

We could always cobble together a few dollars in a crisis, but the kind of money it seemed we needed to adopt a child? Not a chance. She knew I was right.

I felt bad, popping the balloon like that, but it had to be done.

She was dissolving again, head on the table. I was desperate to restore a scintilla of hope, just enough to make things bearable.

That's when I came up with *the Deal*.

Listen, I said, it's October. Let's take a time out until the end of the year. Three months is all I'm asking. Let's set the whole thing aside so we can absorb all this bad news. In January, we'll check out our options. But there has to be a strategy, and some planning. We can't just go off the deep end and get into something we'll regret or can't pay for. Do we have a deal?

The tears were flowing and the pain was bottomless, and I just wanted desperately to shelve the thing for a while.

OK, she said, you're right. We can decide what to do in January. I'll let it go for now. She looked up at me and wiped her eyes and nodded. I'll let it go, she repeated.

I breathed a sigh of relief.

She was lying, but I didn't know it.

# Chapter 5

## *The Oatmeal (Part One)*

THE RULES ABOUT EATING:

First, when we are invited to someone else's house and you are served food you don't like, you will eat it without muttering or squinting and you will act like it is the most delicious thing you've ever put in your mouth.

Second, when you are at home and you are served food you don't like, you will never say *I don't like it*. Instead you may say *I don't care for it*. You will still have to eat the first helping but saying you don't care for it will get you out of having to eat a second helping. It is always rude to say you don't like something that's been put on your plate. Never, ever say you don't like it. Even if you hate it, don't you dare say you don't like it.

My mother could be stretched on some things, but not etiquette. She made it clear she was not going to be embarrassed at the dinner table and so she devoted many years to drilling the rules into our heads.

I was able to obey them with great success, even though I lived overseas and traveled around weird countries where I was subjected to some of the most horrific cuisine ever concocted.

With a tight smile I ingested unidentified animal intestines, oriental spices that would wrench the stomach of a goat, unambiguously rotten fruit, and a variety of meat dishes still bleeding or secreting other fluids. Once, I even ate cheese-on-toast garnished with a large, coarse black hair—after it had been prepared by a German woman who didn't shave her underarms or legs. She sported a sleeveless mini dress, just to make sure we had no doubt about her earthy preferences. As she slid the plate over to me, I saw the hairs sticking out from under her arm, apart from the one that had fallen and was stuck on the toast. Even so, I managed.

I accomplished these steely feats of discipline by reminding myself that whatever it was, it would never be as bad as the oatmeal.

A long time ago, for the first six years of my life, I liked oatmeal. I now consider it to be a member of the vomit family.

This is all because of the time I said I didn't like oatmeal.

———

DAWN BROKE that day with sunshine and happiness. I was dressed and ready for school and had wandered into the kitchen to find Mom putting the finishing touches on a breakfast of bacon and eggs. For some reason, it felt to me like a good day for oatmeal.

Mom, can I have oatmeal please? I asked.

Before she could respond, Dad intervened. No, Son, your mom has already fixed bacon and eggs.

It's OK, said my mom, I will make him some oatmeal. There was a brief parental argument which culminated in my request being granted. That's the way Mom was—willing to buck the system occasionally to bring me that bit of extra happiness.

Dad glared at me—a bit menacingly I thought—over his coffee cup.

Within a few minutes the oatmeal was cooked and presented.

But something remarkable had happened, I discovered, during the preparation of the oatmeal.

When you are in first grade, your body is growing and changing constantly, and sometimes your taste buds change too—often quite suddenly. At some point between the request for oatmeal, the debate over the oatmeal, and the delivery of the oatmeal, I realized that in actuality I didn't like oatmeal anymore.

And so just as the bowl was placed on the table, I said: Mom I think I will have bacon and eggs after all.

There was a loud clink as Dad's coffee cup was returned to its saucer with unnecessary force.

What do you mean you will have bacon and eggs? he asked, at an alarming volume.

At this tenuous point in my development, I didn't grasp that a question isn't always really a question. I perceived—mistakenly, as it would turn out—that this was a time for total honesty, and responded simply—

I don't like oatmeal anymore.

I took for granted that this little miracle of nature—the swift change in my palatal senses over which I obviously had no control—would be appreciated for the scientific marvel it was. Consequently, I was taken aback by the hostile reaction that followed.

Dad stood up and gestured vigorously at the bowl under my chin. You are going to eat that oatmeal, he said. Your mother fixed it *especially* for you, and you are going to eat it. Everybody else was happy with bacon and eggs, and you had to have oatmeal. Well now, you are going to eat the oatmeal.

He turned and left the kitchen, spurting another emphatic YOU ARE GOING TO EAT THE OATMEAL as he walked down the hall.

The happiness of the day left with him, and straightaway a pall of gloom enveloped the kitchen.

Mom gave me a rueful smile and slipped away silently.

ESJ, being her usual insufferable self, arose from her chair to parrot the command, having anointed herself the role of Dad's personal enforcer.

You better eat that oatmeal Jim, she sneered, and walked out haughtily.

And there I sat, all alone with the wretched bowl.

At this juncture there didn't seem to be any good options. If child protective services existed at that time, I didn't know about it. I was on my own. I was going to have to eat the oatmeal or there would be fireworks in the region of my backside.

I stared at it for a long while, hoping it would disappear, or that maybe God would whisk it away like He did Elijah, but nothing happened.

With a sigh, I culled a microscopic portion of the gruel on the outermost tip of the spoon and touched my tongue to it. From the tip of my toes, a wave of revulsion coursed through my body. My spine went into a kind of spasm and the oxygen was sucked out of my lungs. I gagged violently, face flushing, eyes watering.

I can't eat this, I said to myself. I simply can't.

I stared at the clock with growing despair. Dad would be back in the kitchen in five minutes when it was time to leave for school, and it was not feasible to have that bowl of oatmeal still sitting there when he returned. And yet the thought of inserting any more of that hideous mush into my mouth was incomprehensible.

Nauseated from both the oatmeal and the fear of what was to come, I weighed my options. I could try to eat the oatmeal but would certainly get sick and might die. Alternatively, I could just sit here and wait to see what happens.

Or to be more specific, I could wait to see how bad the spanking would be.

And then, as I sat there pondering the inevitable, a brilliant realization came to me: the worst part about spankings was the anticipation, not the pain.

Dad could be counted upon to deliver a competent walloping, there was no question of that. But as I thought back on my considerable experience as the recipient of corporal punishment, I grasped that the dread of what was coming was far worse than the event itself. Typically, there was a prolonged period between the pronouncement that a spanking had been earned, and the actual spanking.

Like for example: You're going to get a spanking when Dad gets home, Mom would say. And that would be hours away—hours during which I would be crippled with anxiety.

Or, if the misbehavior occurred at church, the spanking would be deferred until we returned home. That also involved a dreadful period of trepidation, to say nothing of the embarrassment of having everyone at church knowing what I had coming. They would look down at me pitifully like I had an appointment with the executioner.

But now, here in the kitchen with the oatmeal, I realized the span of trepidation had been compressed to five minutes. And—irony of ironies—school would play an integral role in my deliverance. In five minutes, we simply had to leave. Dad was never late for anything in his life, and we wouldn't be late to school on account of a bowl of oatmeal. Five minutes of dread was nothing. I could do anything for five minutes. And even better, the spanking itself would be rushed. The pain would last for but a moment. It was far preferable to ingesting the bowl of toxin facing me.

It was so simple, so ingenious, so utterly foolproof. And when the five minutes elapsed, it worked far better than I imagined.

Because when Dad returned to the kitchen, it turns out I evaded punishment altogether. He glanced at the undisturbed bowl of oatmeal, stared angrily at me for a moment, and commanded me to the van. I grabbed my school bag and hurried out, careful to maintain an expression of solemnity. On the inside I was gleeful. This was an unprecedented escape.

What happened in there? I thought to myself, as Dad cranked up the Volkswagen van.

Was it an unexpected expression of mercy?

Had he concluded that the deprivation of breakfast was punishment enough?

I didn't know. I just knew I had prevailed, and it was glorious.

---

THAT WAS a fine day at Cannon Hill State School. We were always given a half pint of milk at line up, so that got me through to morning break. There was this little canteen where, between classes, they sold mini boxes of Sunbeam brand raisins for ten cents, and I had squirrelled away a few coins for a calamity like this. I made it through the whole day without suffering any side effects of the missed breakfast. If there were any hunger pangs, they were obscured by the adrenalin of triumph.

When Dad arrived to pick us up, I jumped aboard the van without apprehension. Truth be told, the whole oatmeal war was out of my mind. I was thinking ahead to the sweetest event of every day: after-school dessert.

The second we reached the house we would go bounding up the stairs into the kitchen to enact a delightful ritual that never got old. Two plastic bowls, heaped with ample scoops of vanilla ice cream, would be produced by Mom and placed before us on the table. Then, in a tantalizing routine, a bottle of chocolate sauce would be inverted and suspended over each bowl—when Dad was performing the procedure, from a great height—and a stream of chocolate sauce drizzled over the ice cream.

ESJ would inhale her serving within seconds and be on her way, but I had a special technique to extract every ounce of enjoyment from the proceedings. Using the spoon like a potato masher, I would painstakingly work over my ice cream, mixing in the chocolate sauce until I had a smooth, refreshing bowl of soft serve. By the time this process was completed, ESJ would be long gone, so I could enjoy the experience in total tranquility, without interference. There was nothing so glorious as sitting in the solitude as that sweet, milky confection hit the taste buds and slid gracefully down the throat.

We arrived home and the two bowls were produced on cue. I failed to notice that one of the bowls had been retrieved from the refrigerator until it was placed before me. One when it was on the table did I see that it did not contain ice cream, but what appeared to be withered-looking oatmeal.

A sense of doom came over me as reality set in. The effort to preserve the oatmeal by subjecting it to a full day of refrigeration had certainly not improved anything cosmetically. A crust had developed over the top, and from the ugly brown pallor it was difficult to tell if it was mushy or crunchy. It looked awful enough, but I was hoping I wouldn't actually be eating it. Likely, Dad had saved this specimen to illustrate what happens to food when it is wasted. He was going to use it as an object lesson about ingratitude and mention the starving children in Africa and all that.

But then things took a disturbing turn as he placed a spoon next to the bowl and said, in a chillingly measured tone:

You are going to eat the oatmeal.

Forthwith, ESJ began making loud slurping noises with her ice cream in order to illustrate its deliciousness. A physical assault on her would have been appropriate, but I was fixated on the bowl of oatmeal. This can't be true, I thought.

I'm going downstairs, said Dad. Don't get up until you have eaten the oatmeal.

I sat listless and depressed.

ESJ took twice her usual time making an extravagant production of her ice cream consumption. And then she smiled evilly and departed.

A few moments passed, and I heard the beginnings of play time formulating outside the kitchen window. Kids were laughing, yelling, having fun. And ESJ was getting the Hoppity Hops out.

---

THE HOPPITY HOPS were the crown jewels of the Ray family toy collection. They were inflatable rubber balls with handles, imported from America, brought over in the barrels. You sat on them and bounced around like a jackrabbit. With a little momentum and courage, you could bounce to the stratosphere on a Hoppity Hop.

The best part was that we were the only ones with the Hoppity Hops. You couldn't buy them in Australia. It's not that we were the only kids in the neighborhood with Hoppity Hops

—it was way better than that. We were the only kids on the continent with Hoppity Hops.

They were our passports to unmitigated stardom on Meyrick Street. Kids would flock from all points in the hopes of having a go on the Hoppity Hops. Boys who heretofore were interested in me only as a test subject for their latest Kung Fu moves would see the Hoppity Hops and trip over themselves with overtures of friendship.

ESJ had a red Hoppity Hop. Mine was blue. I was generally possessive of all my belongings, but to a greater degree of the Hoppity Hop, because I knew there would be no replacement if some misfortune should befall it. Never did I allow ESJ to get anywhere near it.

But now as I sat in lockdown—unable to intervene or lodge any grievance—I heard ESJ's voice drifting up from the yard, as she cheerfully said to some unseen neighbor—

Here, you can ride Jim's blue Hoppity Hop. You can use it all day if you want.

Where's Jim?

He's not allowed out today.

Why not?

Because he won't eat his oatmeal.

# Chapter 6

## *The Oatmeal (Part Two)*

On the second morning I awoke to the sweet fragrance of French toast wafting into my room from the kitchen. It had been rough, that evening before. I was hoping it was over now, but doubted it was. I had been allowed to have dinner, but Dad mandated strictly pedestrian fare—green beans, etc., and then it was back to the bowl of oatmeal.

Four hours it had been, sitting at the kitchen table, and I had downed a total of three bites of the stuff. There was a lot more oatmeal to go. To say I had not made a dent in the project would be inaccurate, because there were now three literal dents in the oatmeal from the three spoonfuls I had scooped out. It no longer had the liquidity required to find its own level.

The French toast meant one of two things, I was thinking. The whole sordid ordeal was being deemed concluded, and we were going to celebrate a new, oatmeal-free day. Or, maybe it was another phase of the torture—I would sit there with the oatmeal while being forced to watch ESJ slurp away happily at her own mouth-watering stack of French toast drowned in a lake of syrup.

It was in fact neither. Mom knew how much I loved French toast and had prepared it in the hope it would motivate me to quickly gag down the oatmeal, and then join the rest of the family in a normal breakfast. But when Dad retrieved the bowl from the refrigerator again, I was beside myself. Around the edges, the oatmeal now had the texture of cement, while under the thickening crust, the soft core had developed some curious elastic properties.

The misery of the predicament consumed me and I launched a strategic protest, toggling between self-pity and hostility. I started by wailing about the Hoppity Hop, and then denounced ESJ's efforts to exploit my misfortune.

It isn't my fault I don't like oatmeal anymore, I said, and now it's all lumpy and making me sick, and this whole thing is being blown out of proportion because Joy is making fun of me. And now my Hoppity Hop is going to get burst or ruined or stolen because everything she gets her hands on ends up broken or lost. What am I going to do when the Hoppity Hop is gone? Who's going to get on a plane and go back to America to get me a new Hoppity Hop? No one, that's who. And I'll never have another Hoppity Hop, ever. And it's not fair I have to lose my Hoppity Hop because of the oatmeal. And she shouldn't be allowed to use my Hoppity Hop anyway and I wish you should stop her.

I sensed my lip quivering involuntarily and realized this was the perfect conclusion to the soliloquy, so I let it go on and multiply until I was trembling all over.

That was pretty good, I thought to myself. The injustice of linking a simple bowl of oatmeal to abuse of my personal property and, by extension, threatening my entire sense of happiness. Surely it was a devastatingly effective argument. A more sympathetic figure than me, I could not imagine.

I allowed a few seconds of silence to envelope the room. I

pushed a beautifully timed tear from my eye socket, trickled it down my cheek, and narrowly missed the bowl as it splashed onto the plastic tablecloth. Anyone with a modicum of compassion would be deeply moved by the spectacle.

Then there was a smacking noise from across the table as ESJ reengaged with her French toast.

Dad stood up from the table.

If you don't want Joy to play with your Hoppity Hop, he said, you are going to have to eat the oatmeal. But you need to get one thing through your mule head. I don't care what happens to the Hoppity Hop—it could explode right now as far as I'm concerned—but I do care about this bowl of oatmeal your mom fixed. And you are going to eat the oatmeal.

As he left, Mom made a quick plea for mitigation.

Can he put a little more sugar in it?

One teaspoon, Dad replied, without turning.

The sugar was a mistake, because in order to mix it in I was forced to rotate and expose the moist underbelly of the oatmeal, which triggered another wave of nausea. It was like turning over a fetid corpse. Revolting, unwieldy clods of goo adhered to the spoon, and for the first time now I began to sense the odor of curdling milk.

ESJ made a show of praising the deliciousness of the French toast as we collected our things for school. As I left the kitchen, head drooping, out of the corner of my eye I saw the nightmarish bowl being returned once more to the refrigerator.

―――

It was hard not to think about the oatmeal at school this time. All day long, the specter of what was to come filled me with dread, and I was distracted to the point that I wandered into a caning from Headmaster Scruggs.

Mr. Scruggs was an ill-tempered, egomaniacal twit of a man whose sole function, as best I could determine, was to wander about the school grounds whacking pupils with his cane for minor or imagined offenses.

I had received the cane once before, following a crime in which I was plainly the victim. It happened after ESJ had intervened on my behalf, and as a result of her help I was punished. That's the way it was with her—even in rare instances when she was trying to be nice, things tended to end badly for me.

I was walking into school one morning, minding my own business, when three hooligans hiding behind the front gate pummeled me with dirt clods. One of the missiles opened a gash on the back of my head. I had the schoolyard savvy to know the incident should remain unreported, but ESJ physically grabbed me and escorted me to the headmaster's office, where she presented me and my bleeding head to Scruggs, also divulging the names of the attackers. He adjudicated the matter by caning all four of us savagely across the palms.

After that I was always on the lookout for Scruggs and his cane. But today, distracted by grim thoughts of the oatmeal, I wandered out of line on my way to math and Scruggs materialized from around the corner and lit into my hamstrings with his wand of terror. By the time I could scamper to the proper position in line, four painful whelps were rising from the backs of my legs.

Maybe I just won't go home, I thought. Maybe I will disappear forever, live on the streets, or stowaway in a Boeing wheel well back to America, where there are other people who love me. That will show them. If I never come back, they'll be sorry. I developed the thought for an hour or so and then became hungry. My raisin fund had dried up.

That evening I went for sympathy again with a stirring account of the caning in all its brutality. All I was doing was walking to class, I said. Mr. Scruggs caned me for going to class. I don't even know what I did. Last time I got the cane for bleeding. And now I get it for going to math.

The way I envisioned it, my dad would arise from the table, say the boy's been through enough, head for the fridge, and grab the ice cream.

He went for the fridge, but not for the ice cream.

He wouldn't cane you for nothing, Dad mumbled. Whatever you did, you must have deserved it.

———

I DIDN'T HEAR ANYTHING, but between Day Two and Day Three I think there was some type of tactical discussion between Mom and Dad, because on the third morning my dad deviated from the monochromatic *You Are Going to Eat the Oatmeal* speech to more of a motivational approach.

Son, are you sick of this oatmeal?

Yes, sir.

Do you want to get this over with as bad as I do?

Yes sir.

We all want this to be over. Mom wants it to be over. I want it to be over. You want it to be over.

Yes sir.

It's not bothering me, ESJ interjected.

Dad glanced at ESJ for a moment and then returned to his pep talk.

Today is Friday, he said. Steak night tonight. Ice Cream. Mom's making a pie. I don't want everybody's weekend to be ruined.

Yes sir, no sir, I don't either.

I liked the way this was going. It seemed to be working up to some sort of compromise, for a second.

Well, he said, there's only one way to get this over. You need to eat the oatmeal.

I returned to the amorphous blob and chewed a few bites before leaving for school. There was no doubt about what would be awaiting me when I got home.

---

AT SOME POINT late in the school day, my spirit snapped. I had achieved much in life with obstinacy, but something inside told me this one was unwinnable. I got home that night and proceeded to the kitchen resolvedly and set up a trio of beverages, dilutors to facilitate the ingestion of the oatmeal which at this stage was the equivalent of a putrid granola bar. I chiseled manageable pieces out of the bowl and gulped them down with copious mouthfuls of water, milk and orange aid. When it was over, my parents celebrated as if I had just won the Olympic marathon. I felt defeated and sick. My stomach churned like an industrial clothes washer for hours, but I held it down.

There was a modest victory, which was only revealed in the ensuing years. I was never required to eat oatmeal again. Perhaps that concession was a nod to my tenacity, but more likely was because my mom skillfully maneuvered to prevent another bowl of it ever being placed before me.

---

THIRTY YEARS LATER, my wife and I were standing in the kitchen of my father-in-law Jim. It was a few weeks after January 1, 2000—Y2K—the date on which a worldwide computer meltdown was supposed to have triggered the end of civilization. My in-laws had amassed a formidable cache of food, weapons and ammunition in anticipation of the crisis.

Now that the event had passed innocuously, they seemed mildly disappointed.

We were about to become the beneficiaries of their excessive purchases as Jim pulled endless stores of food from his garage and handed them to Stacey. I was delightedly watching this bonanza unfold until the moment when he emerged with a monstrous canister of oatmeal of the size normally sold only to restaurants, or perhaps armies.

My face evidently registered the sudden queasiness that seized me, because he gave me a puzzled look.

What, you don't like oatmeal?

I was trying to think of how to answer when Stacey—well acquainted with the story of my childhood tribulation—stepped in to respond for me.

It's not that he doesn't like it, she replied. He just doesn't care for it.

# Chapter 7

## *Football*

Getting your face kicked in on the first day is not really the best way to begin the school year, and it didn't help that I was from America and didn't know what team I supported.

This was the town of Corby. It was in the middle of England but half the residents were from Scotland, and they all walked around perpetually livid about generations of injustices thrust on them by the English. Something about how the government opened the new steel works in Corby, and the unemployed came down from Glasgow in droves for the work, then they closed the steel works, and now practically the whole town was on the dole. Always had it in for the Scots, the English did, and they had done a right number on them in Corby.

I didn't really have a complete understanding of the socioeconomic fabric of the region or who was to blame for the multifarious woes of the community, but when someone said they were going to kick your face in, well, I could grasp the meaning of that.

I had only just arrived on the school grounds and was wandering around meekly when the first little Scot tacked menacingly over to me and began jabbering in a bewildering brogue. I captured just a word here and there but got enough to understand the message that he didn't care how tall I was, he could kick my face in any time he fancied it, especially since I was American.

And then he asked a question, delivered in an ominous tone which conveyed unmistakably that my continued health hinged on a proper answer:

What team do you support? he said.

I did not have slightest idea of the meaning of this interrogatory. How do you support a team? Do you send it money? Lift it in the air somehow? Anyway, having only just arrived in the country I didn't so much as know the name of any team on this side of the Atlantic. But sensing the wrong answer could trigger a violent attack, I answered as blandly as possible, saying—

I don't support any team.

He squinted, looking at me as though I were a troglodyte.

Ye canna no' support a team, he countered. Ye must support someone.

Well, I don't. I don't support anyone.

Ye must.

But I don't.

The pressure was building up in his head, and it looked like it might explode.

That's all I can tell you, I said apologetically. So, what team do *you* support? I asked, hoping to divert attention from my ignorance.

Again, the look of scorn.

Can ye no' see the shirt I'm wearing, ye great daft moron? It's Leeds bloody United. I should kick yer face in now.

Baffled, he drifted away. I wasn't precisely sure what had just transpired but was happy to have deferred a beating.

Similar encounters were repeated two dozen times throughout the week, with each inquisitor demanding to know the team I supported. I experimented with the answer of the Dallas Cowboys or Atlanta Braves with no improvement in the reactions. By the end of the week a groundswell of disgust was building up against me, and I began to sense that the innovative tactic of not being able to name any team on the British Isles would probably not continue to have the same disarming effects for much longer.

---

Walking home on Friday I sought counsel from my solitary friend, Kevin. He lived across the street from me and had been trying, with no small measure of exasperation, to acclimate me to my new country. In the first few weeks of our acquaintance, I had taken advantage of his fascination with meeting a real live American to dazzle him with tales of my former life in the States as a gridiron star, boxing expert, fearless hunter, and general all-round hero. It was all a pack of lies, but he had no way of knowing it yet.

Kevin was a pintsized lad with an unruly mop of curly hair and an uncontrollable penchant for amusement to match. He looked for a laugh in everything and manufactured the comedy when necessary. His mind was always working toward the next joke, and you could see the process playing out on his face with the twitching nose and the raised brow and the mischief gathering behind the eyes.

Kevin had only just moved to Corby himself and was also new in school, but as an Englishman knew much more than I did and was proving to be an invaluable ally. He had listened patiently as I arrogantly lectured him on the superiority of American football over rugby, Muhammad Ali over Joe Bugner, and baseball over cricket, even though I knew nothing of what I was saying. Now I needed his help.

Almost got my face kicked in again, I told him. They keep going on about supporting a team or something.

He laughed robustly, to the extent he was unable to remain upright and his ears turned bright red.

Ah, yes, he said, steadying himself finally. If I may offer a bit of advice. I don't know what it's like in America, but football is quite important here in England. Not American football, mind you. Real football. And these Scottish lads, they've no patience for anyone who doesn't show proper support and loyalty. You must support a team, or—yes, quite right—you're going to get your face kicked in massively.

What team should I support, then?

We sat down on the curb. Kevin pondered deeply for a moment, taking in a rare moment of gravity.

Well, there's international, and there's club football, he said. It's either England or Scotland for International. I suggest England.

Why?

Because Scotland is rubbish.

But what about the Scottish boys? If I tell them I support England, won't I get my faced kicked in?

There's always the risk of that, he said, waving a concessionary hand, but there are loads of England supporters at school. Once you select England—and provided you don't wander off alone without your mates—you'll be quite safe. Just don't keep talking about the Dallas Cowboys. Carry on with that and you'll be taking your meals through a straw for the next fortnight.

Now, Kevin continued, in the football league, you can support any team provided it's not Leeds United.

What's wrong with Leeds?

Leeds United, he answered with an air of disgust, they have Billy Bremner, Peter Lorimar, Joe Jordan, Gordon McQueen. All disgraceful players. Hooligans, the whole lot of them, and most of them play for Scotland as well. Complete rubbish. You'll want a side in the First Division with some English lads: Manchester United, Liverpool, Arsenal, Tottenham Hotspur, someone like that.

What team do you support then? I asked.

Here he was thrown off a bit, forced to concede that his team was the lowly Wolverhampton Wanderers, a rather anemic club mired at the bottom of the league table, where they thrashed about constantly trying to stave off relegation. He'd previously lived in Wolverhampton, so he felt compelled to stick with them, but acknowledged there was nothing much appealing about a squad that sported bright orange jerseys and went by the nickname Wolves—while actually playing more like lambs, and drunken ones at that.

When we arrived home, Kevin retrieved a stack of football books from his room along with a dozen recent issues of *Shoot!*, the national weekly football magazine every schoolboy read with religious fervor.

Have a look at these, he said, and watch the Saturday football programmes on the telly. You'll find a team to support. Just remember mate, it must be an English side... division one. He jabbed a forefinger in my direction. Anything from Scotland won't do.

I went home with Kevin's stack of research material and set it on the floor by my bed. I had a brief session of mourning as I accepted the reality I would never be watching Roger Staubach or *Monday Night Football* again. And then I decided to get on with my new education.

———

AT FIRST, my knowledge of the sport consisted only of the general awareness you weren't supposed to use your hands, and I began with the singular goal of learning just enough to avoid an assault. But that weekend changed everything. Once I started paying attention to my surroundings, it became clear why the whole country was raving mad for football. On Saturday morning I went out and learned the basic skills from Kevin and his friends. We had a grand time until I volleyed the ball into the front garden of a psychotic neighbor we called Grizzly. He stormed from his house incensed and confiscated our ball, screaming about trespassing, threatening to call the police and waving a fist for good measure. The English and their gardens.

Then we went in to watch the football preview shows. There were only three channels available in Britain, and one of them didn't even start broadcasting until at least four o'clock in the afternoon, so there were two options for football news.

The British Broadcasting Company's legendary *Grandstand* program was anchored by Frank Bough, a conventional, staid chap who embodied the tradition and stodginess of government television. He was balding and eminently dignified to the extent that one wondered if he worked as a butler on weekdays. ITV—the independent, upstart network that had to get along by selling adverts—broadcast a competing show called *World of Sport* hosted by an excitable fellow named Dickie Davies. The antithesis of Bough, Davies customarily wore a vivid jacket and had an impressive quiff of hair complete with a streak of poliosis, giving him a passing resemblance to Pepe Le Pew in both appearance and demeanor.

Topping it all off was the BBC Saturday evening program *Match of the Day* which played highlights of the day's action. The host and analyst was a lanky Londoner named Jimmy Hill, easily the most fascinating and inconceivable character of the lot. Hill was a good natured, pleasant man who happened to look exactly like Lucifer. He seemed to be always wearing an eerie grin, and with his long nose and pointy chin—accentuated with a Van Dyke beard—the satanic effect was unmistakable.

Jimmy would be talking genially about the football league and this player or that goal or whatever, but watching him you felt you were somehow being furtively beckoned into hell. You almost expected a pitchfork to come sailing through the screen at any moment.

But as I began to learn the game—announcer idiosyncrasies aside—I was completely hooked.

Sunday afternoon I read everything Kevin had given me from cover to cover. I was determined to return to school with a working knowledge of the game, and by Monday morning, I had my answers.

Two teams stood out. One I hated, and one seemed just the type of team I could support.

First, I decided I didn't like the look of Arsenal at all. A flash and dazzle team in London, Arsenal's squad was stocked with haughty-looking Irishmen. They were perennial frontrunners in the league but seemed to have an air of smug arrogance about them. And their kit—the team jersey and shorts—was a complete bore, a bland patchwork of red and white that looked like something someone's mother had sewn together from scraps. I couldn't see myself sporting that outfit to school, and beyond that the very name of the team—which seemed to contain a rude word—was enough to put me off Arsenal entirely.

On the other hand, I liked the looks of Newcastle United, a team with limited successes on the field compared to Arsenal but with a blue-collar ethic that came across as authentic. United's fans were called *Geordies*, a name with origins in the coal mines, it was said. And importantly, Newcastle's kit was striking, composed of authoritative, vertical black and white stripes with a medieval crest in the center—workmanlike and serious but not showy.

And the centerpiece of the Newcastle United squad was an impressive striker by the name of Malcolm Macdonald. He was a square-jawed, solid-looking man with a tremendous set of sideburns, loads of pace, and a thunderous left foot posing a threat to goalkeepers from a range of thirty meters. According to *Shoot!* Macdonald had recently been called up to the England squad where he had thumped in five goals in a single match. Never mind the opponent was Cyprus—the fact was that no other player had managed such a feat in the half century prior.

Best of all, Malcolm Macdonald had an appealing and imposing nickname: they called him *Supermac*.

———

On Monday, as the lumpy school custard was being poured at lunchtime, I was informing everyone within earshot that I was now a supporter of Newcastle United and a fan of Supermac. As fortune would have it—and I would only later discover—the City of Newcastle was very close to the border with Scotland. This geographical feature neutralized Scottish vitriol and thereafter the questions asked of me were much less stressful, such as whether I knew John Wayne or had been to Disneyland.

I had avoided getting my face kicked in, and in the process had discovered something compelling about this game of football. In short order I was scurrying down to the newsagent each Saturday morning to pick up my copy of *Shoot!* and centering weekends around playing football and absorbing the analyses of the butler, the skunk and the Evil One—better known as Frank Baugh, Dickie Davies and Jimmy Hill.

Better yet, Malcolm Macdonald soon made me all but forget American football or baseball even existed. Week after week, I watched highlights of Supermac terrorizing defenders with his powerful shooting and bone-jarring headers. Anytime he got the ball on his left foot, it seemed, exciting things happened. I was utterly mesmerized by Supermac and Newcastle United. I spent hours outside every evening refining my skills, working on my dribbling and shooting. I imagined myself as Supermac, gliding past flummoxed defenders and vaporizing goalkeepers with my unstoppable shots.

*Magic*, the fans would say when Supermac scored. He's completely magic.

It would not be long before Supermac would betray me and thousands of other Geordie fans, but for the moment, he was magic.

# Chapter 8
## *Applying One's Self*

WATCHING YOUR TEACHER GO OFF HER ROCKER WITH THE knowledge that you've caused it is a bit frightening at first. But ultimately invigorating.

It was a stark spectacle with Ms. MacNaughton because she invested enormous effort in trying to cast a dignified, regal quality, but it only took a moment to transform her from the Queen Mother to Sid Vicious. And it was football—always football—that shattered the eloquence.

Every waking moment was becoming devoted to thoughts of football, including the time allotted for education. All the teachers at Kingswood School were appalled by their students' obsession with *the beautiful game*, but it was Ms. MacNaughton who suffered the greatest distress. Football was a puerile waste of time in her mind, and she inevitably became murderously unhinged at the very mention of it.

The trouble started with my school diary. Students were required to chronicle their daily life experiences, and the first thirty minutes of class were dedicated to writing our diaries. We were expected to craft flowing compositions, describing the prior day's activities in Dickensian prose. On Fridays, Ms. MacNaughton reviewed our entries.

The first week of my diary contained some rather pedestrian commentary on my experiences in a new school and a new country—though I decided not to document the many threats on my life from the Tartan Army—and a few observations about the difficulties of adjusting to the dreary English weather. *Well done!* Ms. MacNaughton noted enthusiastically in the margin.

By the second week, my entire life had been recalibrated around football, and so the diary began to reflect my new interests. There were lengthy entries detailing my meticulous process in selecting a team to support, gushing commentary on how much I loved the sport, and other thoughts about how I was eager for school to end each day so I could play football. When Ms. MacNaughton reviewed these submissions, she was aghast. I was summoned to her desk.

Being in proximity to Ms. MacNaughton was an unpleasant experience and an assault on the senses. She applied an astounding volume of perfume and her makeup was veritably caked around a set of beady eyes that fixed on you with dripping disgust.

What is this nonsense? she asked.

It's my diary, Ms. MacNaughton, I responded innocently.

Yes, I can see that, she said, the voice infused with anger. But it's all about football. There is to be nothing about football in your diary, she added, now picking up the little red volume and shaking it at me vigorously. Your diary is to be a record of your own personal experiences, not what is happening in the football league.

I stood placidly, unresponsive.

Sensing I wasn't adequately absorbing the message, she moved in closer.

I don't care about the football league and want none of it! she was yelling now, right in my face. The confrontation had begun at a distance of six centimeters but now she was almost touching my nose. A wave of stale coffee breath drove me back a step and momentarily subjugated the perfume, but she clawed at my forearm and pulled me back in, the fury and decibels still building.

I am fed up with football! she continued, this time turning to glance across the entire classroom toward other miscreants who needed to hear the message. I want you to write about things in your personal life. I do not care about who Liverpool may or may not have thrashed last week. I do not care about Newcastle United. I do not want to read anything about Matthew MacDonald.

It's actually Malcolm, Madam. They call him Supermac.

The helpful correction did little to diffuse the situation. In fact, she was now fully inflamed as she returned to lean into my face.

I have NOT devoted my life to this school for the purpose of producing another pack of football hooligans, she screamed. There will not be another word about football in this diary. Have I made myself perfectly clear?

Yes, Madam.

It was clear to me, the rest of the class, and the students in other rooms a hundred meters away, I imagined.

The next morning I pulled out my diary and tried to think of something else to write. But when I extracted thoughts of football from my mind, there only remained an empty chamber. It was hopeless. There was truly nothing else in my life warranting any mention. It was my genuine and unshakeable belief that the greatest use of my life at that time was to document the happenings in the football league. Yet the thought of MacNaughton bearing down on me again—with the breath, the indignation, the anger—was awful, so I cobbled together a few lines about what I had eaten for breakfast and tea and other banalities.

I carried on with this for several weeks, endeavoring out of spite to make my diary as boring as possible. Inevitably, MacNaughton summoned me before the class for another lashing.

You are not applying yourself, she said, starting out in a calm voice I knew wouldn't last.

I'm doing my best, Madam.

I think you are NOT, she responded. Again came the escalation, and the invasion into my personal space.

The only thing you've written in this diary for the last three weeks is what you've had for dinner.

Yes, but I'm not allowed to write about football, and—

Uttering that word lit the fuse again. A ruler snapped down on the desk sharply and I sensed she was only just suppressing an overwhelming urge to clap me about the ears.

This is disgraceful. Disgraceful! You are not making a proper effort.

Little bits of spittle were catapulted onto my face. There was nowhere else for them to go. I was that close.

I won't have this lackadaisical rubbish, she continued. You must apply yourself. You are not going to be a professional footballer. One day you might be a doctor, or an engineer, or a teacher.

Or perhaps a psychotic, like you, I thought.

She closed her eyes and inhaled deeply, nostrils flaring. Then she took a long look at the ceiling and reconstituted herself, before drilling into me again with the beady eyes.

You must take your mind away from football, she said, having recovered her Queen Mother voice. Kingswood School has never produced a single professional footballer, and I do not think you will be the first.

We'll see about that, I thought. But in my heart I knew she was right.

———

THE REMAINDER of the school term was an ongoing battle of wills. I was reminded regularly I was not applying myself. But at selected intervals—when I could steel myself sufficiently for the altercation that would be sure to follow—I would slip in a football update here or there.

All the while I went to great lengths to convince my parents I was getting on splendidly in her class, but two incidents brought the charade to an end.

The first was the parent-teacher conference. I knew I would be reported as one who wasn't applying himself and was braced for impending disciplinary consequences, although I nevertheless feigned shock when Mom and Dad arrived home in surly moods.

Ms. MacNaughton says you're not trying very hard, my mom said with crossed arms.

She said that? I replied, simulating great astonishment. Are you sure she was talking about me?

You're not applying yourself, I believe was the way she put it, said Dad. And she recommends you be banned from playing football or watching it on television.

I managed to avoid that fearful outcome, although it took promises, begging and gallons of carefully orchestrated tears.

But there was another shattering event, around this same time, over which I had no control. It was announced that Newcastle United was selling their star striker and my hero, Malcolm MacDonald, for the record fee of £333,333.

And to heap insult upon the injury, the club buying SuperMac was none other than the hated Arsenal.

How could he do this to me?

Later in life when a series of girlfriends kicked me to the curb, I realized it was exactly the same feeling.

If only I could have told my diary how I really felt.

---

EVEN NOW, the long arm of Ms. MacNaughton will reach out and touch me on the shoulder whenever I lapse into moments of sloth. The reproach plays back in my head, as lucid as the day it was first screamed into my face. I am transported again to her desk, standing there prostrate as the scolding is delivered full throttle.

You are not applying yourself, lad. You are not applying yourself.

A small consolation is the memory of a weak moment when the old bat almost slipped and said something positive. She was evaluating class essays and called me to her desk. I no longer recall what I'd written, only that I was berated with the usual indictment about insufficient effort. She started with the predictable rant about how football was dissolving my brain, then she removed her glasses and poised them in midair, looking into space thoughtfully as she collected herself.

If you would only apply yourself, she said, you could be a writer. You could write a book, even. But I know you'll never do it.

# Chapter 9

## *Piano Lessons*

I liked the looks of the trumpet.

If forced to play a musical instrument, I wanted it to be the trumpet. There was never any suggestion, mind you, I would have taken a sufficient level of interest to learn it, but that's what I wanted, I thought.

We do not own a trumpet, my dad said. We own a piano. Learn to play the piano first and then we'll see about getting you a trumpet.

I hate the piano, I said.

Too bad, he replied.

You can lead a horse to water, but you cannot make him learn piano, I would make sure of that. Five years of lessons in Australia on the piano had wrought nothing whatsoever beyond a bungling rendition of *Jesu Joy of Man's Desiring*, a depressing arrangement of Johann Sebastian Bach. He probably intended it be played at public executions—perhaps his own after the public was subjected to the composition.

Now that we had moved to England, my dad decided to take another run at it. No trumpet until you learn the piano.

I hate the piano, I repeated. I hated it in Australia, and I hate it here too. Changing hemispheres does not help anything. It's a waste of money.

Your mule-headed attitude stinks, Dad said, but you will learn the piano.

The oatmeal victory was fresh on his mind, probably.

---

For sheer eccentricity, Miss Riddle, the piano teacher, was a woman in a class of her own. She was a curious little relic who lived on the far side of Corby in a bleak row house rented to her by the town council at a reduced pensioner's rate. Her redeeming quality—in the eyes of my parents, certainly not mine—was that she offered half-hour piano lessons for the austere sum of fifty pence.

Every Saturday morning, ESJ and I would be driven across town for lessons with Miss Riddle. While my sister had her lesson first, I would sit meekly in the kitchen which doubled as a waiting room. It was about eight by eight feet in area and the temperature was kept only marginally above freezing. Miss Riddle saw no reason to heat rooms she was not personally occupying.

The kitchen was adorned with an old lime green gas stove, likely installed before the Great War, a similarly ancient fridge, a tiny vinyl-topped table with a single chair, and a few small cabinets, which of course I looked through. They typically held a box of Wheatabix, a commercial-grade construction material masquerading as a breakfast cereal, the obligatory British staple of Heinz canned baked beans—more about that in a moment— and a few other unpalatable items.

The kitchen's predominant feature, other than the bitter

cold, was a swath of truly hideous linoleum covering the floor that could not have possibly been considered tasteful even in whatever era it was manufactured.

Suppose, I thought, some medieval torturer should be resurrected and tasked with designing a chamber whose aim was to literally bore a youngster to death. He would have found himself unable to improve upon Miss Riddle's kitchen.

There wasn't much to do. You could listen to the muffled clanking of the piano lesson taking place on the other side of the door. Or stare at the discombobulating patterns on the floor with the hopes of falling into some type of trance. Or you could just listen to your teeth chatter.

I would sit there awaiting my turn with Miss Riddle, knowing that back home the Saturday broadcasts of BBC's *Grandstand* and ITV's *World of Sport* would be underway, with Frank Bough and Dickie Davies previewing all the day's matches, interviewing the top stars, replaying highlights from the prior week. Great knots coalesced in my stomach as I dwelled on the sad reality that I was missing all of it.

And then ESJ's lesson would end and I would be summoned into Miss Riddle's sanctum, where things further degenerated.

Come in, love, she would say. Every sentence ended with *love*. I did not like being addressed as love.

At all.

Especially by her.

To begin with, the old woman was fairly obsessed with knitting, and the room was teeming with a panoply of improbable items she had created. A normal English codger might knit the odd tea cozy or sweater, but Miss Riddle evidently considered wool to be the solution to every home interior and fashion need ever imagined. There were picture frame cozies, hand-made seat cushions, blankets, caps, scarves, rugs, and stacks of doilies. And Miss Riddle wove these items while she superintended her fledgling maestros. All the time, she was over your shoulder, feverishly working away with the needles.

Let's begin then. Did you practice this week, love?

Nope.

Then there were the oranges. She compulsively gnawed on orange slices, agnostic to the random jets of juice she was spurting onto the necks and arms of her students.

You're not going to improve if you don't put in a bit of practice, love.

I don't want to improve.

Why ever not?

I'd rather be playing football.

And she didn't worry herself about limiting bodily emissions. Beefy and sustained burps were a regular feature of each lesson, and with the steady diet of baked beans there was always an unpleasantness about the air quality. Sorry, love, she would say without an inkling of embarrassment after a powerful outburst, though silent discharges were never accounted for.

I felt it important, as a matter of principle, to make her earn her ten bob. For starters, I established a goal of arriving for each week's lesson with fewer demonstrable piano skills than the week before. And soon I was emboldened by the realization that my obstinance was never going to be reported to my parents, because Miss Riddle wanted the money.

---

MONTHS and eventually years passed as I went in for my weekly sessions, never improving from the week before and frequently regressing. One week I would hammer out a recognizable delivery of *Jesu Joy of Man's Desiring* and then the next week my efforts would be completely incoherent. I spent four years on the Level One book, only briefly advancing to Level Two for a few weeks before Miss Riddle decided I would need to return to Level One.

In my most creative protest, I managed to interject a Jimmy Hill tribute into the venture. Required by my parents to sit at the piano every night for at least thirty minutes of practice, I worked out a regimen to both squander the time and register my disgust with the whole enterprise. As it happened, the theme music for *Match of the Day* was a catchy yet rudimentary trumpet virtuoso, which I discovered could be replicated on the piano employing a single digit, á la chopsticks.

Did you practice this week? Miss Riddle asked hopefully when I entered for my lesson the week after perfecting my *Match of the Day* song.

Yes, I said, with visible enthusiasm.

Well, then, let's have a listen, she said.

I opened the book with a grandiose gesture to *Jesu Joy of Man's Desiring* and hovered over the keys pensively like Vladimir Horowitz. Then I butchered the piece, purposefully missing numerous keys by a mile. I knew it was agonizing for her because from the corner of my eye I saw the knitting needles stop cold.

Oh, dear, she said. If we're being honest, we can't really say that's an improvement on last week, love.

Sorry, I said, with no suggestion of actual regret.

And you practiced, did you love?

Yes, indeed.

You practiced *Jesu Joy of Man's Desiring*?

Didn't say that.

What did you practice then, love?

Shall I show you?

Go on, then.

I lifted a single forefinger dramatically in the air, and then hammered out *Match of the Day*, hitting the keys hard enough, hopefully, to require Miss Riddle to call a tuner.

Well, that's a proper bit of nonsense, she said with despair.

I think it's lovely, I responded.

---

THESE MEMORIES ARE NOW ADMITTEDLY COLORED with embarrassment, regret and thoughts about what might have been had I applied myself. But then the recollection of a singularly traumatic interaction with Miss Riddle is a reminder that despite everything, I was the true victim.

I was going about my lesson, thrashing about on some painful composition for the thousandth time, when I sensed movement from behind. At first, I thought she was just leaning strategically for another round of flatulence, but presently it became manifest there was something more.

Never mind me, love, she said. Carry on.

There was rustling, several grunts, and the swish of pantyhose.

I turned, to my everlasting regret, to see what was happening. Miss Riddle had removed her pantyhose, right here in my presence, and was standing there in her knickers as she reached for a pair of slacks hanging nearby.

This was the low point of my entire existence to that point, and possibly still. There I sat, separated involuntarily from the football action, and forced into a dank, doily-festooned room where an antediluvian woman was spitting citrus and performing a striptease behind me.

Not long after we thankfully moved back to America, and my parents finally gave up on making me a piano player. It was no great tragedy—perhaps easier for me to draw that conclusion since it wasn't my fifty pence invested weekly. But I can still play *Match of the Day*.

# Chapter 10

## *A Stoppage of Joy*

THE BLEEDING AND BURNED MAN IN THE SHREDDED clothing materialized every night in my dreams. Nightmares, I should say.

I closed my eyes and there he was, staggering around in the tall grass, engulfed in suffering and bedlam. Just beyond him a towering pyre consuming the carcass of the Pan Am 747 he'd escaped moments earlier, still filled with its perishing human cargo.

He went for a holiday and got hell instead.

You can look at a thousand photographs but every once in a while, one will grab and hurt you—and when you are eleven years old, invade your unconsciousness, even, and evoke genuine terror. That's what this one did from *Time* magazine. I can still see every little detail. The worst aircraft accident ever, they said, a collision of two jumbo jets on the island of Tenerife. A thick fog, a hurried pilot, a few misconstructions among people who spoke different languages, and 582 people incinerated.

I didn't know who he was, the bleeding and burned man,

but he was one of the lucky ones. Why him? I wondered. Sitting there in his first-class seat, probably thinking happy thoughts about the sand and the surf when the roof was torn away over his head, the sky awash in grinding metal and jet fuel and flesh and flames.

Somehow, God only knows how, he scrambled away from the carnage, tattered and broken but alive.

To this point I had managed quite nicely on the mantra that *God will take care of you*, like the old hymn says, but here was *Time* with this gory pulp of a man.

There was providence or there was coincidence. Things happened by divinity or by chance. I didn't know which one it was, not after seeing that horror. Some people believe God has His hand in every little thing. Or maybe there is no God at all, and even if there is a God He clearly couldn't be bothered with jumbo jets.

I slept only fitfully for weeks. Enough of this, I thought to myself one night as I lay there in fright. I got out of bed and went into my parents' room, woke my dad and told him I was scared.

I don't understand about the plane crash, I said. I close my eyes, and I see that man from *Time*. If there is a God, why would He let it happen?

Dad got up and we went downstairs to talk. If he minded that it was two o'clock in the morning, I couldn't tell.

It's not an easy question to answer, said my dad. Everyone asks it, sooner or later. Even people in the Bible, like Job and David, didn't know the answers. And Jesus himself said there would be suffering. The best we can do, he said, is trust that the suffering on earth is really nothing compared to the happiness we have ahead of us in heaven.

We can't really see the whole picture now, he said. Someday, though.

He saw I wasn't totally satisfied, but he prayed with me and it helped a little bit, and we went back upstairs and I went to sleep.

---

A FEW NIGHTS LATER, the bleeding and burned man in the plane crash came back. It seemed like whatever he might have done in his life, right or wrong, what happened to him was way out of proportion. And all the other people too—the ones God didn't take care of. Charred to a crisp.

I told my dad it was still bothering me.

A couple of days later he called me into his home study. It was lined on all sides by thousands of books, most of them theology. He had read all of them—most of them more than once, and you could tell because they had his notes in the margins and various passages underlined and circled. To me they were dense and incomprehensible.

Dad could debate anyone of any creed on the grand themes of the universe or on the most intricate points of doctrine. And if compelled to do so would usually have his opposite number in sixes and sevens in short order. But he was at heart a storyteller.

I sat down across from my dad's desk and he told me about a nineteenth century Englishman named J. Hudson Taylor. It didn't seem to have anything to do with the plane crash.

Taylor would become a renowned missionary in China. No one else had given any thought to taking the Christian faith to the East, or starting schools, or introducing modern medicine, or fighting the opium trade. Taylor had this idea maybe God was telling him to do all those things even though people told him he was crazy, or that it would never work, or that he would be killed, or all of the above.

## A Stoppage of Joy   63

At least it seemed like God was telling him these things, but Taylor wasn't really certain. He had his doubts, for sure. It wouldn't do to travel overseas only to discover the voices in his head were not really from God, because in that era they had a penchant in China for removing the heads of people who didn't fit in, usually after protracted and imaginative torture sessions.

So before leaving, Taylor put himself into a series of situations that would allow him to test whether God was really in it or not. Providence or coincidence, he had to know.

A lot of peculiar things happened to Taylor to build up his faith bit by bit, but things really culminated for him in a stinking slum in the city of Hull. He was apprenticing for an absent-minded physician whose memory was particularly deficient on paydays. Taylor went weeks without getting his salary. But under the scheme he had devised, God had to be trusted to provide—without any interference other than prayer. So Taylor decided that reminding the doctor about his wages was out of the question.

One Sunday night Taylor took inventory and realized he was down to his last coin and his last meal. A half-crown in his pocket and enough porridge in the cupboard for one more bowl was all he had. In this very moment of rising desperation Taylor was approached by an impoverished Irishman who begged the budding missionary to come pray for his dying wife. His whole family was starving, in fact.

Taylor wanted to help, but then he thought about his own crisis. And then instead of compassion, he felt anger toward the man for allowing his family to get in such a situation.

Somehow or other there was a stoppage in the flow of joy in my heart, Taylor wrote later.

He followed the Irishman into a grungy courtyard and realized he had been here before. Just a few days earlier, he'd been cornered by thugs who shoved him around and told Taylor if he ever came back, they would do him in properly. A flutter went up his spine, but Taylor tamped down his urge to take flight, ascended the staircase and entered the dirt bag of a flat. Four or five poor children stood about, he wrote, their sunken cheeks and temples all telling unmistakably the story of slow starvation. And lying on a wretched pallet was an exhausted mother, with a tiny infant thirty-six hours old—moaning rather than crying—at her side.

Looming large in Taylor's consciousness was the last coin in his pocket. He wanted to relieve this family's distress, but not at the cost of all he possessed.

He kneeled to pray for the family, but the words came out all hollow and hypocritical. He spoke of a kind and loving Father in heaven, but all he could think of was his half-crown. Without it, he might not be eating in the foreseeable future, and yet it was quickly becoming an emblem of faithlessness and duplicity and condemnation. Here he was telling this starving family to trust God, and yet he wasn't willing to part with his last coin. Taylor choked on his prayer and rose.

You see what a terrible state we are in, the Irishman pled. If you can help us, for God's sake do.

Taylor put his hand in his pocket and slowly withdrew his coin.

You might think this is a small matter for me, he said, but in parting with this coin I am giving you my all.

As Taylor walked back home that night, his heart was as light as his pocket. Not only was that poor woman's life saved, but he realized somehow his life was saved too.

The next day as Taylor ate his last bowl of porridge, the postman arrived with an unexpected letter. The writing and postmark were smudged, and Taylor couldn't make out the sender. He opened the envelope and a gold half-sovereign slipped out and clanked on the ground.

In twelve hours, a four hundred percent return on his investment.

Putting that coin in the hands of a desperate Irishman was only a small opening act in the great drama of Taylor's life, but it seemed to forever settle the question of providence and coincidence in his mind. And this despite the fact he would suffer as much, or maybe much more, hardship than the bleeding man in Tenerife.

———

This is the way life works, my dad said. God sends rain to fall on the righteous and the unrighteous. What's important is not whether rain will fall, but whether you will trust God with what you have—or don't have—in every predicament. Faith is only faith, Dad said, if you still have it when it seems to make no sense. Or when you don't think God is listening. Or even when people are getting bloodied and burned.

Dad got up from his desk and came around and hugged me and said a little prayer for peace. I didn't understand everything, but the nightmares faded away.

## Chapter 11

## *The Meow Machine*

A CLUSTER OF THE BOYS TRAIPSING BY MISSED IT, BUT THE one lagging just behind was the one to spot it, lying abandoned there on the curb, unbelievably. There was a glimmer in his eye as he quickly and discretely looked around.

No one else had seen it. Brilliant.

A twenty pence coin, calling his name. He swept back a wave of his mop and moved toward it, trying to maintain an aura of nonchalance.

Across the street—behind a sliver of curtain in the bay window—was my dad, the Right Reverend Mr. Ray, watching the scene unfold, a little grin gathering.

The youngster bent down to retrieve his treasure. A quick scoop, a sweep of his hand into a pocket, and he would be on his way, magically endowed with funding for a couple bags of crisps or maybe some sweets. He went down for it, but it wouldn't budge.

It was stuck to the curb.

For a moment the lad crouched there, befuddled, and then something in his head told him this wasn't possible. He dug at it a second time, then a third. Now he was on his knees, confused but determined, clawing away at the coin that—this couldn't be true—was somehow affixed to the concrete. Five minutes later, tormented and defeated, he finally moved on, glancing back repeatedly with incredulity. The man behind the curtain was elated.

Next morning the boy was back with his mates, this time a team effort. They couldn't move the coin either. Dawning was the reality of a cruel trick, but how? They looked around vainly for the orchestrator, vaguely suspicious they were being observed and ridiculed. But it was twenty pence. You can't abandon twenty pence without giving it everything. Again though, failure, and the group slinked away in dejection.

Superglue.

It was new on the market and not many people knew about it. But Dad did, and his first thoughts upon learning of this miraculous substance were not about what could be repaired, but how it might be utilized to augment his vast repertoire of practical jokes.

He was a paradox of a man, and the pranks came off with spectacular success in England because of his dignified station as a man of the cloth. Very few people went to church anymore, but there was nevertheless a pervasive notion that all vicars were dull and humorless clumps. It was regularly reinforced by their appearances on BBC television documentaries, force-fed to students at school, in which one primeval minister or another would drone on endlessly about William of Wykeham or Archbishop Thorseby or the intricacies of excommunication. They made no effort to make the stories interesting or trim nose hair for the cameras, and they most certainly never smiled.

From a distance, Dad looked every bit the reverend draped in propriety. He could not abide casual wear, did not own a single pair of blue jeans or shorts, and wouldn't think of going out in public without a tie, at the very least. In one memorable episode he was taken ill at home, fever raging and blood pressure plummeting to the point of threatening his life. At some time between when the ambulance was called for and when it arrived, he crawled unseen into his bedroom—crawled, literally—and put on a suit, so as to be presentable as a Man of God in the emergency room. The paramedics assured him the hospital had no dress code and, in point of fact, they had never even transported a patient with a pocket square, but the argument was lost on him.

Yet behind the veil of formality, he was always planning his next trick, and those who saw only a stuffy minister were at risk of being waylaid.

———

THE SUPERGLUE WORKED wonders in the seventies, but in the eighties he discovered an even more effective, if unlikely, tool with which to enrich his hobby: the 1981 Plymouth Champ. This was after we moved back to America, and Dad was traveling all over the country for speaking engagements and growing increasingly frustrated by the exorbitant cost of fuel.

When he decided to trade an unwieldy Oldsmobile, I presumed he would return from the dealership with something at least marginally cool, but despaired to see him roll into the driveway in the Champ.

It was Lee Iacocca's answer to the Chevrolet Chevette, even though it seems inconceivable now anyone would have been asking the question. The Champ was truly a pathetic vehicle. Ugly, constructed of low-grade plastic, slow, and bereft of any positive features except that it would go forty miles on a gallon of gasoline. And the name *Champ* was pointedly ludicrous because the thing was a lightweight deathtrap that would have surely come out second best in a collision with any other vehicles on the road, including bicycles.

But when Dad purchased some aftermarket equipment for his Champ it was forthwith converted into an outstanding prankwagon. The key accessory was a powerful public address system, installed discretely under the hood, capable of perforating the eardrums of anyone in the vicinity. The element of surprise multiplied the effect because the Champ was about the most innocuous looking vehicle on the road, if it was noticed at all.

After experimenting on hundreds of innocent pedestrians from every angle with an assortment of unusual noises, my dad determined the most effective sound effect for generating sudden fright was a protracted and deafening MEOW. He had owned scores of cats as a farm boy growing up and now it was going to pay off, for he had perfected a haunting feline cry.

If you don't think a MEOW can terrify, it's only because you've never been subjected to one delivered at 130 decibels, right behind your head, without warning.

By the time he involved me in this enterprise, Dad already had the system beautifully refined. We were in Kokomo passing through some nondescript neighborhood when he spotted a middle-aged gent, walking innocently down the sidewalk, his back to the Champ.

Dad turned the volume on the P.A. to 10 and picked up the microphone. Watch this feller, he said, but try to act normal when he looks back at us, like you didn't hear anything.

At a range of fifteen yards—
MEEEOOOOOOOOOOOWWWW.

The counteraction was epic, and cascading. First, the shock wave launched the old boy vertically straight up. In a fraction of a second—still airborne but now on the way down—his brain began to process the sound, and the only possible thought in that moment of horror was likely that a fifty-foot-tall cat, maybe larger, was upon him and poised to attack.

Reaction, part two. Feet returning to terra firma, he spun around, lifting an arm as he turned in a defensive gesture to deflect the massive claw surely about to sweep across his throat. As this happened, I saw his face for the first time, his features screwed up in a tight grimace. The countenance utterly stricken, as one would expect from someone facing eternity on short notice.

Part three. As the scene came into focus for him, he realized with relief that somehow, there was no monstrous beast pouncing. There was nothing at all. Just two guys passing in a Champ who didn't appear to have heard or seen anything.

Part four. Well past the victim now, I discretely craned my head to look back over my shoulder—a passenger side rearview mirror wasn't included with the Champ—to watch the finale. He was now in a haze, having pivoted every which way without seeing any sign of the predator. And then, just as he was fading from our view, he looked down at his feet, perhaps formulating the only remaining viable question:

Am I going crazy?

This was quality entertainment and we never tired of it. Sometimes on road trips it was rerun a hundred times in a day. Rolling along city streets Dad would spot a candidate walking and invariably reach to power up his accessory.

Let's try a meow on this one, he would say.

Mom, when she was in the Champ, complained. She was thoroughly embarrassed by the Meow Machine, and worried Dad would be arrested, that his ministry would be scuttled if word got out, that an unbalanced victim would be pushed over the precipice or—most of all—that someone would have a heart attack.

You have to stop this, she would say, over and over. This is not a good example for the kids, and you could kill someone.

You're probably right, Dad would answer, but then he would spot another target ahead and reach for the irresistible microphone. Just a couple more meows and we'll be done.

I do not know how many victims were subjected to this treatment, but they would number in the thousands and are scattered from Miami to Minneapolis. More in the North, because he preferred targeting Yankees. There must be people out there like the man in Kokomo, still pondering what it was, that day they were milliseconds from death, but survived to scamper home in soiled undergarments.

Why? I would imagine his wife asked him when he arrived home.

I was walking down Sycamore Street, and there was this giant cat bearing down on me, but when I turned around it was gone.

The Champ only lasted a few years, it being a Plymouth, and I was sad to see it go. We tried to duplicate the meows with subsequent vehicles, but they never quite worked so effectively. Dad fell back on his other schemes, which included sending fake letters of complaint to other pastors from alleged disgruntled parishioners, doctoring photos in his home darkroom so that colleagues would appear to be in compromising positions, utilizing Hugo—a ventriloquist dummy with a positively satanic countenance—to terrify the children of friends, and miscellaneous other gags involving electric shocks, squirting water, talcum powder and various other substances.

———

THE BOYS on the street eventually realized who was behind the twenty pence piece, although they didn't understand how.

After a long struggle, they looked around, and spotted him receding behind the curtain.

It's that bloody American vicar, they said.

There was nothing more to do but deliver a gaggle of long-bowman salutes toward the window, and then they capitulated and slunk away.

My friend Kevin and I were watching this from the back of the room, utterly dissolving on the floor.

Best twenty pence I ever spent, said Dad. And then he went promptly into his adjacent office, closed the French doors, and began studying for his sermon. In mere moments, he was deep into a commentary, reading scriptures to himself out loud, deadly serious, practicing to get the inflection just right for Sunday.

Your Dad is—, Kevin said, looking through the glass and pausing as he worked out a way to say it without giving offense.

—he's a bit unusual for a reverend, isn't he?

## Chapter 12

## *The Kingswood Senior Centre*

A PANG OF GUILT JABBED AT ME, STANDING THERE WITH the youth choir at church as we practiced our song, the grand old hymn *He Leadeth Me*. I think Kevin felt a bit remorseful, too, but only a bit. Not enough to stop what we were doing.

He leadeth me, he leadeth me, the song goes.
*By his own hand he leadeth me.*
*His faithful follower I would be,*
*For by his hand he leadeth me.*

I knew it was wrong for me to be singing *He Leadeth Me* considering what we were doing with the mudballs.

The mudballs made going to school exceedingly more interesting. There were two logical routes from our neighborhood to Kingswood Primary School, and because we normally went home for lunch, it was a roundtrip made twice daily. One way was to go up Colyers Avenue and then straight across on Kingsbrook street, which ran through a spiffy neighborhood of detached homes.

The second way wasn't as direct but a bit more appealing— via a little fenced pathway that weaved around some back gardens, along a ridge overlooking the Kingswood Senior Centre, and then gently up the hill to school.

Kevin and I walked to school together since we lived on the same street and by traveling in pairs you didn't have as much worry about getting your face kicked in by some roving representatives of the Tartan Army.

Also, Kevin was incapable of going five minutes without creating some form of entertainment. He eschewed boredom, even on a five-minute jaunt to school. And everyday life could be greatly enhanced, he had discovered, with mud.

Say what you like about the quality of healthcare or cuisine in England, but there's absolutely no denying they have fantastic mud. The constant precipitation and mild temperatures collaborate to create a fine, malleable substance perfectly suited for many forms of mischief. The supply is unlimited. And in the hands of the practiced schoolboy, it has more uses than WD-40.

Kevin, I would soon discover, had learned to use it to great effect and to really put an edge on things, he liked to target the same victim repeatedly.

From the first day of school, Kevin was reconnoitering potential victims. There was a man residing on Kingsbrook Street who presented an irresistible mark, for the reason that he showed every indication of having an obsessive disorder about his vehicle. The first time I saw him—hunched over his gleaming Triumph 2500 with cloth in hand and a canister of wax perched on the bonnet—I knew he was going to be in for it.

He looked to be the sort of gent who had little going for him in life except his car. He was mostly bald on top, save a circular clump of hair on the frontal lobe he had nursed compensatively into a long wave. As he vigorously buffed away, it swung wildly from its mooring and flapped about his face. His wool sweater rode up the back, exposing a polyester shirt which never quite stayed fully tucked. He was a man, I supposed, who much preferred spending quality time outside with his motor vehicle than passing the time inside listening to his wife drone on over tea and biscuits. This element of his life—and probably only this element—he controlled and mastered.

But he couldn't be outside all the time.

The first attack was a discreet trial run, just to assess the subject's level of attentiveness. Gliding innocently past the Triumph one morning, a perfectly formed mud ball cupped in hand, Kevin nonchalantly stooped for just a flash and affixed it to the front license plate, then quickly recovered his gait.

When we came back by at lunch time, the mud ball had been wiped clean with no sign it had ever been there.

The next day Kevin walked past the Triumph some distance before swiveling and launching three missiles, two sticking nicely to the windshield and the third donking loudly on the roof. Unable to resist participation now, I added a fourth and fifth contribution to the project. At lunch time, once again: all of them gone.

There was some discussion during the course of the day—between spontaneous bouts of uncontrollable laughter—regarding the propriety of our activities. We acknowledged it was wrong and could lead to a lot of trouble, but the exhilaration overwhelmed any thoughts of quitting.

As we approached on the morning of day three the gentleman was on guard, standing in his front garden, arms folded, fixing us with a suspicious glare. Confident we hadn't been seen in the act, we bid him a cheery good morning. He smiled faintly but continued to eyeball us as we continued down the street.

I think he's on to us, I said. Perhaps we should start going the other way to school.

Nonsense, Kevin replied. He only knows it's happening in

the morning. It could be any one of a hundred people walking to school.

We'll have another go at lunch, he said confidently.

And indeed we did. Lunchtime came and with the owner nowhere in sight, the Triumph was again impressively renovated with mudballs.

Over the next two weeks the assaults continued, and with four trips along Kingsbrook road daily, we varied the time and manner of delivery to avoid detection and inflict maximum distress. Mudballs were splattered on every conceivable surface of the car. The owner made ever more frequent appearances in his front garden looking increasingly frantic as the days passed. Whenever he was present, of course, we passed by innocently.

One day he opened his gate and came out to intercept us and have a word.

I say, lads, he said. I've had a bit of trouble with hooligans defacing my car with mud. Do you know anything of it?

I tried to appear concerned about his troubles while disavowing any knowledge of the matter.

Bad luck, that, Kevin said with a touch of sarcasm that didn't go undetected.

The man's eyes sharpened a bit, like a lawyer who knows the witness is lying but lacks proof to the contrary.

Well I must tell you, he said, I've never been so cheesed off. The police have been called, and it's going to be curtains for whoever's involved when they're caught.

I gulped discretely as we turned to continue our journey to school. The warning had me rattled enough to again urge a suspension of the activities.

Kevin was unaffected. The police! he said mockingly. He really expects us to believe he's phoned the police over mudballs? What a load of rubbish that is. The police have more serious things to concern themselves with than this pathetic bugger and his car getting a bit of mud on it.

A few more days passed with the car owner diligently on guard at his front gate, morning and evening, rain or shine. He had now reached the point where he was largely suspending his entire life to watch over the beloved Triumph.

And then, one morning he was curiously absent. Nowhere to be seen. A wave of adrenalin coursed through me as we prepared to resume hostilities.

I told you he couldn't keep it up, Kevin said as he began to knead another of his special creations. We came upon the car and from point blank range Kevin garnished the windshield again.

I had my arm cocked to deliver an additional embellishment when the gent suddenly materialized from behind a rose bush in his front garden, as if launched from a spring. He was coming at us on a dead sprint with murder in his eye.

We bolted from the scene as he gave chase. You little horrors! he was yelling, but the voice quickly faded as we left him behind. My heart pounded as we rounded the corner a hundred meters distant. I glanced back to see he was trailing badly, but still coming at a full trot.

We hustled into the school playground and quickly advanced to the far end, blending into a throng of students. The Triumph owner was now standing at the fence, face crimson, shirttail hanging, scanning the crowd.

He stayed until the bell rang but never spotted us, and with great relief we scurried inside behind our human shield.

That was too close for my liking, I said, still puffing. We have to stop this.

Kevin agreed. In principle.

The next Sunday we were at church looking ever so innocent, again singing *He Leadeth Me* and proclaiming that whate'er we do and where'er we be, still 'tis God's hand that leadeth me. The old feelings of guilt came back, and I was thinking about my mom's admonition that your sin will always find you out, and I knew we couldn't carry on.

But it was loads of fun after all and in the end we compromised and decided we would leave the Triumph man alone and find a different victim. We avoided Colyers Avenue altogether and switched to the second route to school, which took us around the back side of the Kingswood Senior Centre.

---

IT TOOK ONLY a few moments of surveillance to realize this new course was very promising indeed.

The Senior Centre was a sparkling new facility, built by the government to gently ease pensioners into the sunset of life. Usually, these places were depressing old monstrosities, but this one was nicely done with its oversized glass panes and lovely landscaping. The large windows allowed passersby a view into the world of the codgers. Inevitably, there would be several of the residents sitting docilely, napping or staring absently at the television. An attendant or two could occasionally be seen meandering around tending to their needs.

Best of all, the footpath passing the Senior Centre was atop a rise running the length of the building. We commanded the high ground and would be firing downhill. And should we be chased by anyone, the pursuer would have to negotiate a climb up muddy terrain just to reach the path, and there was no defilade to allow the type of surprise that had almost got us captured before. General Montgomery would have appreciated the tactical advantages.

Kevin quickly took a knee to gather some muck. He scooped up a few fingers full and gently molded it into a smooth sphere, about the size of a golf ball. Quickly perusing the area for observers, and seeing none, he launched the missive toward the Senior Centre. The mudball climbed in a majestic arc and seemed to hang forever. Then it silently descended toward its target, landing on the window with an almighty, succulent thump.

Even from here, on the hill, we saw the glass reverberate slightly with shock waves as the missile hit the mark and attached itself firmly to the window. The sound of the attack would surely have caused alarm inside but as I turned to congratulate Kevin, I saw he was already twenty meters distant, accelerating away from the scene. I quickly followed.

We hit it again on the way home, and over the next few days it became evident that mudball removal at the Senior Centre wasn't nearly the high priority task it had been with the Triumph. They collected over several days, drying on the windows until they were rock hard. Soon, the building looked like it had been machine-gunned by a platoon.

And then, after about a week, we saw him. This time the protagonist was the maintenance man. We rounded the corner one morning to see him six rungs up a ladder, bitterly scraping away at the now cement-like dollops.

He was a slender fellow who looked very much like Stan Laurel—gangly and wearing a permanent expression of bemusement—and we were relieved at the sight of him. The feelings of guilt were assuaged now because we had confirmation the clean-up wasn't burdening the actual residents. This gentleman was on the government payroll and would be working anyway.

If I'm honest, we're doing him a favor, said Kevin. Now he has the opportunity to get a bit more fresh air and exercise.

In the following days the attacks became increasingly brazen, with Stan the maintenance man cleaning the windows at weekly intervals. Compared to the Triumph owner, he seemed lackadaisical. Eventually, though, he figured out the mudballs were much more troublesome to remove after they had dried and stiffened. He began to monitor the situation, watching us out of the corner of his eye as he tended to other duties. Still, whenever he wasn't seen to be on guard the mud balls were sent flying upon his facility in appalling quantities.

Yet the status quo was never acceptable to Kevin, and one day he made the decision to attack while Stan was actually on his ladder removing mud from the prior day's assault. We had just passed by and given him a friendly wave, and I had given up thoughts of attacking. But Kevin suggested we double back and really liven things up.

Perched as he was on his ladder, Stan didn't see us return. He seemed to be entranced by his work, muttering a profanity or two as he scrubbed away. We quietly prepared two mudballs each and then launched them almost concurrently. All four projectiles sailed inexorably toward the mark, which happened to be the window next to the one he was cleaning at that instant.

THU-WHUMP.

THU-WHUMP.

THU-WHUMP, THU-WHUMP.

It must have been a terrifying moment. The poor man shot straight up six or eight inches, nearly jumping out of his skin, then flailed desperately, limbs groping for something solid. He took a deep breath, enjoyed a moment of relief and then—recalling what had instigated his wild ride—was filled with wrath.

The invective was coarse and hateful, and featured several words I had never heard. And then he was down the ladder and up the hill, after us with alarming swiftness.

We couldn't lose him, the rage driving him faster than his

normal capabilities. We entered the school premises with only a twenty-meter gap. But here, local knowledge would save the day, as we whipped around a series of corners and diverted through obscure hallways until Stan had no hope of finding us. And then we laughed until very nearly wet ourselves.

Stan, though, had had enough. Even while we struggled to compose ourselves, he was at the headmaster's office lodging a grievance.

After morning assembly we trudged to class, which began ominously as the teacher, Mr. Fell, retrieved a note from his door box.

I have a memo from the headmaster, he said. Someone has been plastering the Senior Centre with mudballs and it says here there is reason to believe the offenders are students at Kingswood School. The caretaker has followed two individuals who disappeared onto the school grounds before they could be detained.

He looked out over the class disdainfully.

I don't even have to ask who is responsible for this, he said.

My heart plummeted into the lower regions of my stomach as I closed my eyes and waited to hear my name called. But then, unexpectedly, the name that sprung from Mr. Fell's lips was neither mine nor Kevin's.

David. David McGrory, he said. I know it was you, I have no doubt whatsoever. Off you go at once to the office.

The explosive denial was instantaneous. McGrory stood up and threw his chair against the wall, utterly enraged.

I've got nothing to bloody do with it, he yelled. I know nothing of it. I don't even go near the place.

You can take that up with the headmaster, Mr. Fell retorted, waving an index finger toward the door. You are an absolute disgrace, Mr. McGrory. Off you go, now, or you'll only make things worse for yourself.

A surprising development, this was, but I soon worked out what had happened. David McGrory, a freckled, red-headed little brawler of a Scot, was a genuine demon and had a disciplinary record to fill volumes. He was always in trouble and usually at the epicenter of any act of vandalism. It was only natural he would be assumed to be the culpable party.

This time he was actually innocent, but the only people in possession of this salient fact were me, Kevin and the accused. And certainly, neither Kevin nor I felt compelled to intervene. We sat quietly—and greatly relieved—as McGrory left the room in bitterness.

As I understand it, things got much worse for him when the interrogation got underway with the headmaster, because he was immediately called upon to divulge the name of his accomplice. Stan had been clear that two boys were involved. McGrory refused to answer and of course had no idea what they were talking about. His protestations of innocence should have carried some weight, because normally McGrory freely admitted his criminal activities, often in advance of committing them.

Eventually he was sent back to class after Stan said he looked like one of the culprits but couldn't be altogether sure. McGrory wasn't punished but remained under a cloud of suspicion.

In the ensuing days he was on a mission to find out who was to blame for this troublesome episode in his life, and it was at this point that we became genuinely fearful and swore off the mudballs forever.

We hadn't told a soul of our involvement, which was lucky because David McGrory was quite capable of killing us on the spot. He was a maniacal junior felon who seemed normal at times but could instantly snap and produce stunning levels of brutality. He constantly initiated fights and had never lost, even though he routinely challenged older boys twice his size. And once his opponent was reeling, the sight of blood would send him into a complete frenzy. Just recently an older lad had come down from another school for the purpose of exacting retribution for his younger brother, whose nose had been smashed by McGrory on account of some minor disagreement. In no time at all, the avenger found himself beaten into unconsciousness by McGrory, who then continued the attack by stomping on his head as he lay prone on the ground. It was a grim, terrifying scene which ended only when teachers arrived to pull the mad Scotsman away.

Kevin and I were on good terms with him but knew what would happen if he found out we had let him take the rap for the mudballs. In fact, he laid it out his intentions with precision.

Whoever did this, he announced to the entire class, is going to have their faced kicked in. And then they are going to have their dad's face kicked in. And their mum's face kicked in. And their dog will be set on fire.

Given he had already been arrested the prior year for trying to burn down a neighbor's house, we accepted the threat on its face.

This is getting quite unpleasant, Kevin said on the way home, and there was a quiver in his voice. We went on to other forms of amusement.

Luckily, David McGrory never learned the truth. We avoided getting caught, per se, but there were still a few consequences to bear. The long and circuitous trips to and from school on yet a third route—necessitated by the need to avoid the crime scenes—soon became tiresome.

---

AND THEN SHORTLY BEFORE CHRISTMAS, when I had just about forgotten the whole sordid ordeal, the director of the youth choir—who, as it happens, was my dad—felt it would be wonderful if we would share the love of Christ by singing carols in the community.

He knew nothing about the mudballs and is only learning about them just now, as he reads this.

He could not, accordingly, have anticipated my consternation when he made the announcement to the youth choir about the upcoming schedule.

I'm delighted to tell you, said Dad proudly, that we have been invited to give a Christmas concert at the Kingswood Senior Centre.

# Chapter 13
## *The Kiss*

I was kissed by Gretchen and then we moved back to America. Those two things changed my life.

My recall of these events, however, is disparate. The flight back I remember clearly—window seat on a blue and white Pan Am 747 from Heathrow to Dulles.

Of the kiss, I have absolutely no memory.

I was fourteen when Gretchen and her family came to England on holiday and stayed with us for several weeks. I felt an inexplicable need to impress Gretchen, and thus spent the entire time of her visit exposing her to my now vast knowledge of English football history. For some reason, she stayed close by me and endured it for hours on end.

It was only after Gretchen left that ESJ, taking a break from her vigorous program of mental cruelty, explained to me that Gretchen had a crush on me, and I was a numbskull for having been blind to it.

I was very skeptical about any relationship advice from ESJ. This was, after all, the same person who only months earlier had surreptitiously signed me up for a pen pal relationship with an exceedingly unappealing Dutch girl, and the first I knew of it was the day I received a letter from Eindhoven composed in jagged English and accompanied by a personal Polaroid. ESJ had taken the liberty of writing a letter on my behalf, signing my name for me, evidently suggesting I desired to form an ongoing postal relationship with a girl on the Continent. In truth my interest in the Netherlands extended no further than the exploits of football superstar Johan Cruyff and the performance of their national team in the World Cup. I was mortified by this fraudulent misrepresentation, which naturally delighted my sister.

Nevertheless, when ESJ began to recount details of Gretchen's recent visit, highlighting little encounters that would suggest she liked me and vice versa, I was compelled—reluctantly mind you—to credit my sibling nemesis with switching the light on in my head.

Sadly, at the moment of illumination, Gretchen was long gone.

Many years hence, Gretchen informed me she had kissed me in an elevator on the day of her departure. It should have been a watershed moment, an unforgettable point of amorous awakening. And yet I curiously have not the slightest recollection of it to this day. My brain, misfiring under the strain of utter juvenile bewilderment, expunged the entire incident from memory.

---

SHORTLY AFTER THIS experience and the gradual realization that ESJ had been right, we moved back to the United States and I found myself equipped with a sudden interest in girls. At the same time, though, I became acutely aware of the fact that like many eighth graders, I was steeped in nerdiness and not remotely attractive in any way.

Exhibit A was my lanky, emaciated, pubescent body.

Rest assured, I recognized this was by no means the only problem, but it certainly was the most obvious. Girls, I was sure, would view me from afar and immediately scamper away before having the opportunity to contemplate other disqualifying flaws, such as the total inability to engage in normal conversation, gauche mannerisms, a robust case of acne, difficulty walking, and so on.

I resolved to do something about my body, and quickly. In this I invested grave contemplation and planning, feeling my very life depended on it. Standing before the mirror one May evening, I took stock of my deplorable assets.

Slumped, wafer-thin shoulders. Not the slightest indication of any chest muscle. Fully visible ribcage—front, back and sides. Classic twig arms. And, worst of all, an incongruously large set of buttocks.

It was an unsightly image, but I was almost encouraged because it would make the coming changes so much more dramatic. By the time I started at my new school in America, girls would be inexorably drawn to my imposing physique which would feature immense biceps, bulging pectorals threatening to burst free of my shirt, rippling stomach muscles, and Earl Campbell thighs.

Now all I needed was to decide upon the best strategy for building this tour de force of manhood, posthaste.

I started with weight training in the garage, but that proved to be problematic. First, workouts there generated ridicule from ESJ, who would make frequent trips downstairs to mock my efforts. Second, I learned solo weight training could be dangerous after I spent approximately three hours trapped under a barbell while attempting to establish a personal record on the bench press.

Far too embarrassed to call for assistance, I lay there helplessly, able only to roll the bar back and forth along my torso, crushing various vital organs. When I finally escaped, I ambled back up to my room, desperately wondering if there might be a better way.

I was still throbbing a few days later when the latest issue of *Inside Sports* magazine arrived in the mailbox, leading to a fortuitous discovery. Buried in the back pages among other advertisements, I discovered the answer I had been looking for, and his name was Charles Atlas.

I had never heard of Charles Atlas, but he seemed to know all about me.

I don't care if you are skinny or fat, Mr. Atlas said, I am ready to help you now!

Judging by the accompanying photograph, he was certainly qualified. Tanned, strapping, forceful, surrounded by women. The leopard swim trunks were a bit unusual, but I wasn't looking for fashion advice. And if I was impressed by his physique, I was wholly awestruck when I read his story. This powerful specimen of manliness had once been a skinny weakling, ashamed of his ninety-seven-pound body.

He had once been just like me.

The next day, I mailed the coupon requesting more information from Mr. Atlas. He was quick to reply with a letter informing me that for an investment in the neighborhood of forty dollars—which by happy chance approximated my life savings—I could become a student of the Charles Atlas *Dynamic Tension* Course.

There were more photographs, stirring testimonials from previous students, and a promise that if I ordered and paid the first installment right away I would also be furnished, as a free bonus, booklets on the secrets of jujitsu, hand balancing, and amazing feats of strength—such as how to pull a locomotive using only a rope and your own brute power.

I hadn't previously contemplated the necessity of pulling a locomotive. But since now it had been brought to my attention, it seemed like if the situation ever presented itself, any women in the vicinity would be thoroughly mesmerized.

Best of all, no weights were needed, the course could be completed in the privacy of your bedroom, and the program was designed for busy people who didn't have all day to work out.

Of course, as a junior high student beginning summer break I did, technically, have all day to work out, but didn't want to. Especially now I knew it wasn't necessary. By the time I reached the end of the letter—which Mr. Atlas impressively signed, *Yours for Everlasting Health and Strength!*—I knew my world was about to brighten.

It was clear Charles Atlas and his course was everything I needed. Other fools could spend all day grunting with weights if they so desired, but not me. I would be in my room secretly building my Charles Atlas body, free from the harassment of ESJ or anyone else.

Your mirror will become your friend, said Mr. Atlas in his promotional materials, and I was positive he was telling the truth.

The first course arrived, along with Mr. Atlas' pledge to mail additional courses every ten days. I jumped in with raging enthusiasm. Every exercise was illustrated in photographs by Mr. Atlas, clad only in the ever-present leopard shorts.

The first course focused on building a massive chest. Certain this would be accomplished within the ten days, my only concern was that I would develop the massive chest before receiving the additional courses covering other body parts. For example, I worried about the prospect of a massive chest accompanied by the twig arms, which might look odd. Nevertheless, I knew as long as I continued to send the payments, Mr. Atlas would faithfully send his courses, and by summer's end the picture would be complete.

As time passed and more courses arrived, it became increasingly difficult to overlook the fact that many of the pictures looked, well, dated. Mr. Atlas seemed to have an unusual proclivity for Brylcreem, which was hardly in style. And some of the women who flocked around him in those beach photos appeared to be wearing swimsuits from a bygone era.

And yet I would shake off those concerns and forge ahead. He may have been on the eccentric side, but the photographs did not lie: Charles Atlas was indisputably all man.

Day after day I stood before the mirror, performing the secret exercises. I concentrated. I strained. I followed all the instructions.

I *believed*, I well and truly did.

I carefully examined every muscle group, anxious to document the slightest improvement.

And absolutely nothing happened.

The massive chest did not materialize within ten days nor at any time thereafter. And as the summer evaporated, the mirror did not become my friend. I was forced to the conclusion that Mr. Atlas was simply in over his head when it came to overhauling my body. He hadn't understood the scope of my situation.

―――

HE HAD OFFERED A GUARANTEE, but I didn't ask for my money back, afraid that embarrassing questions would be asked. (*Dear Mr. Ray: Sorry that Dynamic Tension couldn't help you. To verify your complaint and receive your refund, please send a photograph of your pathetic, gaunt body—preferably naked. I will post it on our bulletin board so that my very attractive all-female staff can mock your image every time they visit the water cooler.)*

In the waning days of summer, I happened upon the shocking truth while rifling through the *World Book* Encyclopedia. Charles Atlas had expired in 1972 at the age of seventy-nine.

The man who was promising me everlasting health and strength had himself been dead for the better part of a decade.

Somehow, Mr. Atlas had neglected to mention in any of his courses that he was deceased, or that his methods were older than my grandparents. Once again, I had been victimized by fraud.

The body I took to the ninth grade was no different than the one I had taken from the eighth grade, except that I now had more acne and less confidence than ever before.

There was little reason to hope I would ever be kissed again.

# Chapter 14

## *The Larramore Scratch*

I WAS EXCITED ABOUT MOVING TO AMERICA. They had Doritos and Cap'n Crunch and Dr. Pepper and more than just the four channels on the television.

Also, I would be going to a Christian school. No more worries about getting your face kicked in every day or teachers blasting you with atheism and pontificating endlessly about the arrogance of Americans. And thanks to the gulf in skill levels between continents I would be transformed instantly from below average footballer to virtual superstar. For once, I felt I would fit in perfectly.

Naturally, this feeling was swiftly and emphatically crushed.

On the first day.

I already realized the Bible had quite a few rules, but when I arrived at Tennessee Temple Academy it became apparent there were scores of others I had somehow overlooked. Fortunately, school administrators were on hand to set things right in my head.

There is a scripture that says people look at the outward

appearance, but God looks at your heart. At Temple Academy they focused on the outward appearance but claimed it was from God anyway. And they had specific rules about your outward appearance, which was scrutinized endlessly. Drift ever so slightly from the guidelines, and you were in trouble with school officials, who would instantly diagnose you with a heart problem, and an attitude problem on top of that. You need to *Get Right with God*, was the way they said it. Get Right with God or get out.

The first sign of trouble was an admonition from fellow student Millard Hibbits that my hair was too ungodly long, and a detention was imminent. Millard was a nerd among nerds who had gravitated to me within minutes of my arrival, attached himself like a leach, and appointed himself my new best friend and personal advisor.

I really did not want anything to do with Millard. Even though I was in no danger of being mistaken as a member of the cool kids' faction, I could certainly detect nerdiness when it was being emitted at nuclear levels.

Walking down the hall with Hibbets clinging to my side that first morning, I noticed many people—girls in particular—physically retracted as we approached. Quasimodo would have enjoyed warmer receptions than this kid, and little wonder why. At least the Hunchback had the good sense not to wear checkered, high-water polyester pants, jacked up above his hips to expose striped tube socks. And whoever was responsible for cutting Hibbets' hair (his mother, it was later revealed) had a streak of cruelty. The hair cleared his ear by a solid inch, the most extreme set of whitewalls ever seen outside Parris Island.

I need to speak with you privately, Hibbets told me after the first class. In a stern voice, he informed me, man to man, that my hair length was unacceptable, and I was going to be in big trouble when the authorities noticed. It shows you have a bad attitude, he said.

My hair was already short enough, I thought. It might not have been up to Marine Corp standards but it's not like I was modeling Shaun Cassidy. I dismissed Hibbets' counsel as mindless nonsense.

---

LATER THAT DAY we went to chapel service where I got my first look at the bizarre pair of martinets who ran the school with an iron Bible. The vice-principal was Dr. Braxton, an intimidating, beefy character who had embraced the crew cut as a fashion statement in the early forties and had never seen any reason to change. The principal was Dr. Winters, a man who looked like Dennis the Menace but operated like Attila the Hun, albeit always with a smile.

After a sermon largely composed of browbeating and reminders that most of us were not even remotely near being Right with God, Winters abruptly asked the teachers to cover all the exits.

We are going to have a hair check, he said, and get this semester started out right. All young men will enter through this door to my right. Don't even try to sneak out another exit.

Presently I was funneled into a gauntlet which had Winters at its terminus, where he was inspecting every student's hair. Next to him was a notepad-wielding assistant taking names.

The hair check procedure involved Winters grabbing a tuft of hair from the side of the head and yanking it down forcefully to see if it could be made to overlap the ear from any angle. This level of scrutiny was needed because of the worry that, once off school property, students might brush their hair in a different direction, if possible, so that it would cover part of the ear.

People who are Not Right with God, that's the sort of thing they do.

Hibbets, ahead of me in line, breezed through inspection, but I didn't make it. Winters jerked at my hair, sneered, and took my name. On my first day, I had inadvertently run smack into the preeminent creed of Temple Academy.

The Doctrine of Hair.

Many religious institutions fussed about with the more traditional Christian doctrines, such as the Doctrine of the Holy Spirit or the Doctrine of the Last Things. With a bit of duplicity you could bluff your way through Tennessee Temple Academy without ever embracing those, but you were never going to escape the Doctrine of Hair.

The essential element of this doctrine held that long hair and facial hair of any kind was an affront to God. The Apostle Paul had written that long hair on a man was shameful. Scripture left a degree of uncertainty in reasonable minds about what might be technically considered long, or whether the prohibition was really applicable in the twentieth century. Temple Academy administrators, however, were experts at eliminating ambiguity. They had determined that if any hair touched any part of a man's ear or his collar, then he was in flagrant violation of scripture, assuredly Not Right with God, and in need of harsh and immediate correction.

I had heretofore been unaware the Apostle Paul even wore a collar, and where they got the bit about facial hair being sinful I was never really sure. You know, what with Jesus having the beard and all.

I wasn't unduly concerned about my detention until I started hearing troubling accounts about what it actually involved. It wasn't an afternoon study hall, like at most schools.

It required sitting ramrod straight and motionless for an entire class period.

It didn't seem humanly possible for any eighth grader to go almost an hour without moving, certainly not me. It will be torture, people told me, sympathetically. Literal torture.

That night on the way home, we stopped at the Pioneer Barber Shop to bring my hair into compliance.

What is it you need? the perplexed barber asked as he ensconced me in a sheet and reached for his spray bottle.

It has to be off my ears, I replied.

It is off your ears, he said.

Yeah, but I go to Temple.

Oh, I see, he said knowingly. There was an unsettling click as he discarded the attachment from his shears and—following an extensive search in some deep recess of a cluttered drawer—replaced it with a smaller one.

The man took to his job with troubling enthusiasm. I tried to suggest some nuance, but he'd heard the word Temple and gone into full boot camp mode. The result was horrifying.

---

Day Two at school involved a relentless stream of mortifying comments about my haircut. For perhaps the only time in his academic career, Hibbets went the whole day without suffering any abuse. The entertainment possibilities offered by my head and its vast swaths of exposed, whitewashed scalp commanded my classmates' full attention.

In chapel, Dr. Winters gleefully read out the detention list. As my name was called, countless eyes turned toward me, producing more embarrassment. Public humiliation was a significant element of the Doctrine of Hair.

The final bell came all too quickly. Now the hell would start.

A wave of fear coursed through me as I approached the appointed classroom. The proprietor of detention hall, Mr. Dick Adams, was a skinny, bespectacled fellow sheathed in a royal blue polyester suit, which I would later discover he wore every day of the week and twice on Sunday.

He had his head down grading homework papers, and as I entered timidly he didn't bother to look up but simply waved a vapid hand, motioning me toward a desk.

This can't be all that bad, I thought, taking my seat. The man didn't look unusually menacing.

Six or seven other miscreants walked in, also victims of the spontaneous hair check.

On the wall above the teacher's head, the long hand on a cheap plastic clock was about to hit its apex.

Three o'clock.

Mr. Adams set down his pen, leaned back, clasped his hands behind his head and monochromatically rattled off his rules which he had long since memorized.

Welcome to detention hall, he said. Detention begins now and lasts for fifty minutes. Keep your feet flat on the floor. Hands on the desk. Don't talk. Don't chew gum. Don't stretch. You may not move any part of your body except your eyeballs. Don't fall asleep. You may blink, sneeze, sniffle or cough. Don't make any unnatural or objectionable noises. Violate any of these rules, and you fail. You will not be told if you've passed or failed until the end of the hour.

You are allowed five scratches, Adams continued. Six scratches and you fail. I—and I alone—will keep a count of your scratches. If you have a question, raise your hand. A question counts as a scratch. If you ask me how many scratches you've used, I won't tell you, and it will count as a scratch.

He leaned forward and picked up his pen to resume grading.

I've been doing this a long time, he added. And yes, I have eyes in the back of my head. If you think you're smarter than me, be my guest.

And then, silence.

The room was oppressively hot and sweat began to bead and make runs down my back. Places that had never itched begged to be scratched. Knuckles cried out to be cracked. Spiders, I'm quite certain, crawled along crevices all over my body. Stomach muscles began twitching involuntarily and the desire to extend my legs became an obsession. A crick developed in my neck. I wondered what the consequences would be if I jumped up and ran out of the room screaming. This was all in the first two minutes.

My original assessment of Mr. Adams as a pliable lightweight was quickly disabused. He was a despot wielding the power of life and death. Periodically he would get up and walk around, stretching conspicuously and making a point of demonstrating just how glorious it was to have the freedom to move about. I imagined him riddled with bullet holes. Or cut apart with a scythe. Or set on fire in his polyester suit, which surely was flammable. It helped a bit, but not enough.

Somehow I stayed still, motivated by the grim knowledge that failure would mean a repeat visit to detention hall the next day.

It was the worst hour of my life. I was a wreck when it ended, but fully committed to the Doctrine of Hair. I was also reassessing whether I really wanted to live in America anymore.

———

I would make several future appearances in detention hall, but always for infractions that had nothing to do with my hair. And fortunately, I was able to break free from Millard Hibbits and fall under the tutelage of R.D. Larramore, an intellectual rebel who thrived on provocation and never met a rule he couldn't manipulate. He once, for example, consumed an entire Civics class arguing that Jimmy Carter was the finest president in the history of the United States, just because he knew the teacher and entire faculty supported Governor Reagan.

With his fine analytical mind, R.D. realized that Mr. Adams' rules were so specific, they created loopholes for someone with enterprise and mettle. R.D. came up with a scheme that what would come to be known as the Larramore Scratch.

An ingenious exploitation of the rules it was. R.D. would claim to have a severe case of athlete's foot. To execute a scratch on his sole would require bending over, untying his shoelace, removing the shoe, scratching, replacing the shoe and retying the lace. During this elaborate procedure, which was conducted in slow motion and with great deliberation, Larramore would take the opportunity to stretch all the major muscles in his neck, back and legs. This whole process to complete a single scratch could be extended for three or four minutes and would, in aggregate, burn up fifteen to twenty minutes of the detention.

Under this brilliant system, the fifty-minute detention became five epic scratches spaced between relatively short periods of manageable stillness.

The first time he tried this, Mr. Adams tried to fail him on the basis he had moved his head during the scratch. But Larramore appealed his case to higher authorities, arguing convincingly that simple physics mandated that restrictions on moving other body parts must necessarily be suspended during a scratch.

The Larramore Scratch helped me through several detentions, but once it became widely known and adopted by others an addendum to the rules was added: *Scratches must be natural, of short duration, and may not involve removing shoes or any item of clothing.*

Larramore spent the rest of his high school career devising other masterful schemes to taunt the administration while remaining, technically, in compliance. He remains a legend among his former classmates.

Sadly, R.D. was subsequently dealt a cruel blow. Whether it was coincidence, fate, or God's mighty hand of judgment, no one can say for sure, but the poor man went bald almost at once upon reaching the age of majority. Thus he was never able to experience the glory of a long flowing mane.

It is no great surprise that he is now a successful lawyer.

## Chapter 15

### *Any Yard for $12.95*

He wasn't one for going into debt, but through some unusual circumstances one summer Dad had managed to rack up a balance on his Visa. It was driving him crazy. He hit upon the idea of cutting grass to retire his obligation and recruited me to partner in the enterprise. He may also have been motivated by disgust, watching me whittle away afternoons watching reruns of *Mr. Ed*, *Green Acres* and even, in moments of acute boredom, *Petticoat Junction*.

This is how the ill-fated Ray Lawn Care Company was established.

We'll do it together, he said, and split the money. One of us will handle the mowing, and the other one will do the edging.

I'll do the mowing, I said. I always hated using the edger because I tended to edge the skin right of my ankles.

Dad designed a very striking flyer and had them printed. You would think we were real professionals, at least until you saw our equipment consisted of a budget Craftsman push mower and low-end electric weed eater lugged around in the trunk of Dad's 1979 Buick Riviera.

The only thing about the flyer bothering me was the part that said we would cut and edge any yard for $12.95.

Any yard for $12.95? Why are we saying this? I asked.

It's simple, said my dad. The going rate for a yard is about fifteen bucks. We'll undercut the competition by a couple of dollars and make it up on volume.

But what about all these houses around here with the huge, monstrous yards? I argued.

Ah, that's the trick, Dad said. We're only going to put the flyers in mailboxes at houses with small yards that look easy to cut.

Beautiful, I said.

We spent a Thursday afternoon driving around distributing hundreds of flyers. Per the ingenious business plan, we bypassed any yard that looked remotely challenging.

This will be like taking candy from a baby, I was thinking. I allowed myself a few moments of fantasizing about walking into Zayre department store, nonchalantly pulling a thick roll of bills from my pocket and buying every game cartridge ever made for the Atari 2600.

The next day the phone calls started rolling in. I took down names and addresses. We'll be there this weekend, I promised, confidently showcasing my developing baritone.

---

Six o'clock Saturday morning we loaded up the Riviera and headed out. We pulled up in front of the first house on my list.

Are you sure this is the house? I asked.

Did you get the right address? Dad responded.

Yes, I'm sure I did.

But this isn't one of the houses we gave a flyer to, he said.

No, it isn't, I gulped. No way on earth would we have put a flyer at this residence.

I didn't like the looks of this. This house, in fact, was barely visible, because it was looming atop an impossibly steep hill ascending from the street and obscured by all manner of scruffy vegetation.

Can we just leave? I asked, the panic welling up in me. I don't want to cut this yard.

Just then the owner, a large, powerful Grizzly Adams-looking dude, emerged from his garage and promptly greeted us as saviors.

I really didn't think ya'll would come, he said, but I'm glad you're here. I would cut it myself but I've got a bad back. And for $12.95, I couldn't pass this up.

No kidding.

I was trying to figure out what to do, Grizzly continued, when my neighbor over yonder gave me this here flyer. I didn't get one for some reason. Maybe you skipped me somehow.

Maybe so, Dad said. I wonder how that happened?

There was nothing to do but get on with the job. Grizzly retrieved a lawn chair from his garage to watch the proceedings as I tackled the sadistic hill. For three hours I battled the unwieldy Craftsman and its spinning blade of death, heaving and shoving desperately to keep the thing from flipping on me and shearing off a limb. Because the incline was so steep there were large patches where grass refused to grow, and I was regularly enveloped by great dirt storms whipped up by the mower. Exposed roots, huge weeds and rocks seemed to reach up from the very earth to choke the blade and snag my ankles. In short order my flimsy right arm was devastated from a hundred yanks on the pull cord.

When the nightmarish job was finally complete I was so pummeled I could hardly walk back up the hill.

Dad collected our check for $12.95—no tip, of course—and told Grizzly we deeply appreciated his business, but we weren't sure our busy schedule would allow us to cut his yard on a regular basis.

As we pulled away in the Riviera, I looked up and happened to see the man effortlessly slinging four by eight feet sheets of plywood from the bed of his pickup truck into his garage. Bad back, indeed.

Let's hope the next yard works out better, said Dad. After gas, that one worked out to about a dollar fifty each per hour.

---

I WAS TIRED, but instantly buoyed upon arrival at the home of our second customer. It was a quaint little clapboard house and the yard looked measly, little more than a postage stamp. A narrow picket fence ran along the property line, passing just a few feet outside each side of the house. The very sight of it breathed new life into me.

I tried to suppress a smirk. This was more like it. I almost felt bad about charging for this one.

A fragile looking lady answered the door and, just like Grizzly, seemed delighted to be engaging the services of the Ray Lawn Care Company.

Just cut the area inside the fence, she said, and that will be just fine.

The Craftsman sputtered back to life and I had her front lawn completed in minutes. The elation was building into a crescendo as I maneuvered around to the side of the house. That's when I saw her back yard for the first time or, more precisely, some of her backyard. The picket fence ran endlessly into the distance, and darn near disappeared over the horizon. I stared, unbelieving. From where I stood Dad was little more than a speck, trimming around the pickets far away.

The back yard was flat enough, but booby-trapped with an assortment of chains, spikes, discarded lumber, bottles and cans —all hidden under an impenetrable mat of weeds.

Endless hours of misery followed. When it was finally over, Dad again advised our client that with our full calendar, our return was doubtful.

Even if it hadn't been getting dark, we couldn't physically have gone on. We drove home and lurched into the house. I collapsed on the floor, where I would remain for many hours.

How many yards did you cut today? Mom asked.

Two.

Two?

Yes. Two.

But you left at six o'clock this morning, and it's dark.

We know. Let it go.

---

IN THE HORRIFIC weeks to follow, many more of the *Any Yard for $12.95* flyers made their way into the wrong hands. I was ready to concoct any lie whatsoever to get out of the jobs, but Dad had too much character to back away from a guarantee. No matter who called, we cut their yard at least once. And eventually, we did get some easy jobs and turned them into repeat customers.

Then the death threats started coming in.

Is this here the Ray Lawn Care Company? The voice on the line was youthful but menacing.

Yes, how can I help you?

This is our territory over here in Ringgold. Ain't nobody but us cuts grass over here. If you know what's good for you,

you won't bring none of them flyers over here no more. Stay out of our neighborhood and quit taking our business away. We'll stop you any way that's called for.

Still we carried on, now cutting yards nervously while keeping an eye out for snipers. There's nothing else in life to match the exhilaration of cutting a five-acre, snake-infested yard on a steep hill, in one-hundred-degree heat, for half of $12.95, while expecting—every single moment—to be sprinkled with buckshot.

The retribution never materialized, thankfully, and we survived the summer. When it all ended I had fresh insight into the challenges of entrepreneurship, a busted Craftsman mower with a million miles on it, and Dad had his Visa paid off. The Ray Lawn Care Company, its mission accomplished, was duly liquidated.

The next year I received several calls from a bevy of undesirable customers imploring me to return to cut their yards. None was more persistent than Grizzly Adams, who still had his flyer and went to the extent of framing his request as a charity case.

I'm real bad sick, he said, and I need some help.

I'm sorry, I said, but I've taken a better paying job.

And though I would have been quite willing to lie, my demur was in fact true. I was working the summer at a print shop for the minimum wage of three dollars and ten cents an hour. It was comparatively glorious.

# Chapter 16

## *Getting Right with Brother Melvin*

Woody Woodfin stuffed a last quadrant of pimento cheese sandwich into his mouth, stood up from the lunch table and made his declaration.

We ain't going forward. We ain't going forward and that's all there are to it, he said, voice inflected with defiance. I gave him the thumbs up. With that settled we trudged from the lunchroom and across the street to the chapel.

Moments later we sat placidly in the pews as Brother Melvin Duckett advanced on the pulpit. It was Friday, the fifth and final day of the school revival campaign. The preacher bore a visage of grim determination. He meant business this time. I glanced toward Woody, who returned a slight nod, reaffirming the agreement. Under no circumstances whatsoever would we succumb to the altar call.

Days one through four of the revival had not been a success in the eyes of Brother Duckett—measured, that is, by the only statistic of importance to him: the number of students responding to the invitation to come forward and Get Right with God. They had gone forward, actually, in droves, but Brother Duckett had set the bar high—he wanted every last one of us. On the first day, in the opening moments of his sermon, he had announced commandingly that God would touch every heart. There would be no exceptions.

And therein lay the rub, because Woody and I were resolved not to give him the satisfaction. Four days of pontificating had worn down most of the student body. Most of them realized it was a numbers racket and had concluded, not unreasonably, that the sooner they ambled forward to Get Right with God, the sooner Brother Duckett would load up his Airstream and leave town, and then things could get back to normal. By the last day, there remained only a smattering of holdouts.

Chief among the resisters was our classmate Barlow Barrett, an enigmatic young man widely deplored by the faculty for his refusal to exhibit any spiritual inquisitiveness whatsoever. In an environment where capitulation was expected, Barrett stood alone as an immovable object.

Most students had a button somewhere capable of being pushed by a manipulative teacher to elicit the desired response. For some, there was the fear of parents receiving a call from Doctor Braxton about a bad attitude. For others it was the excoriating classroom lecture about rotten apples spoiling a barrel. The rotten apple in question might not necessarily be mentioned publicly by name but would be fixed with a withering stare from the teacher while the matter was under discussion, making the subject of rebuke plain to all. Still others feared—or it was suggested to them—that the Lord would remove them promptly from earth if they became of no use to Him, and failure to go forward on the invitation was prima facie evidence of uselessness. One way or another, pressure could be brought to bear.

Pressure could be brought to bear on everyone except for Barlow Barrett, it seemed. He was supremely intractable, employing a variety of strategies generally calculated to tender the impression that he did not possess a soul. From the opening bell of our daily Bible class, Barrett would mentally and quite visibly check out to pay a prolonged visit to some other dimension. Eyes glazing over, Barlow would place himself in a trance-like state, mitigated only by the rhythmic chewing of aspirin. He claimed to enjoy the taste—said it was a delicious alternative to Life Savers or chewing gum—and this quirk only bolstered the impression that something was horribly askew deep within his reprobate head.

When called upon to open class in prayer, which was not optional, Barrett had the unsettling technique of delivering a monochromatic intercession with his eyes wide open while staring impassively out the window or looking around the room. When confronted for this sacrilege by one teacher, his riposte was unassailable, if not necessarily appreciated: Jesus said to watch and pray, he replied, and that's what I'm doing.

So as Woody and I steeled ourselves for the chapel assault we looked upon Barlow with no small degree of admiration.

Whatever happens, said Woody, gesturing toward our exemplar, you know he ain't caving to go forward. If he can hold back, then so can we.

———

Presently our dialog was interrupted by the ardent voice of Brother Duckett. For some of y'all, the evangelist began, this may be your last chance ever to Get Right with God.

It was just starting, but already he produced a handkerchief and mopped his brow.

Brother Duckett was a stem-winding blimp of a man; a profusely-sweating, humorless, bellowing multi-chinned revival preacher wedged in a shiny suit that had ceased to fit many fried chicken platters hitherto. His messages were a collection of fiery admonitions with a single unwavering theme: the lethal dangers of listening to rock and roll music. And the way Brother Duckett preached it, virtually all the evil ever perpetrated anywhere in the universe could be traced back to somebody somewhere playing rock and roll.

We already knew, on our own, that rock music wasn't particularly wholesome. Its promotion of sex, drugs and rebellion was not exactly veiled. The untimely demise of scores of musicians was a matter of public record, and even most of those still alive generally had the appearance of sunken-eyed cadavers.

But Brother Duckett was set to go light years beyond the manifest evidence.

His messages invariably included an exposé on the insidious practice of backmasking, the rock industry's diabolical conspiracy to brainwash America's youth. Each day of the revival, Brother Duckett would present an audio snippet from an LP played backwards and recorded onto a cassette. He would periodically pause the tape and translate the gobbledygook for us—a crucial exercise since the recordings were unintelligible and sounded like dolphins being mutilated.

You young people need to understand, he had cautioned on the first day, waving a forefinger out across the auditorium, that your brains are far more powerful than you can ever imagine, and these devil worshipers have devised ways to subconsciously fill your head ... indoctrinate you with sinister messages designed to destroy your lives.

Brother Duckett pronounced the word destroy with the

accent on the first syllable. *Dee-stroy.* It shaded the warning with a greater gravity. And it wasn't just the lyrics, he said. As we listened to the powerful, mesmerizing beat, we were unwittingly being programmed like a Commodore 64 to systematically commit all manner of nefarious acts.

As the week wore on, we debated Brother Duckett's claims at the lunch table. If anything, he was creating a greater appetite for the music by fixating on it endlessly in his messages and setting it up as the ultimate iniquity. And further, we doubted the average rock musician would have the genius or discipline to execute such a scheme. It was just too complicated for people who, by and large, lived in a dope-induced haze round the clock. In the end, we concluded the preacher's allegations were surely over the top.

If this subliminal manipulation thing is real, Woody said, I should be asking Mr. Compton to backmask his Bible class lectures for me. I'm pulling a low D listening to it forward.

It's hard to argue with that, I said.

Monday Brother Duckett had opened with a few bars of Queen's classic *Another One Bites the Dust* which, we were informed, actually said *It's Fun to Smoke Marijuana* when played in reverse. As the revival continued we progressed through the works of the Beatles, Led Zeppelin, AC/DC, the Eagles, and others. Brother Duckett savaged them all, documenting the allegiance of each group to Satan and providing anecdotes to illustrate that the music would bring immediate and irreparable ruin to each listener.

He had been traveling all over these United States, building a dossier of unusual crimes, accidents and deaths. Over the course of several days he asserted rock music as the proximate cause of, in no particular order: fornication, drug addiction, smoking, laziness, Satan worship, several incidences of matricide, heart arrhythmias, poor academic performance, excessive fidgeting, suicide, certain types of hemorrhaging, migraines, disobedience, arrested development, and a significant proportion of automobile accidents.

In one peculiarly giddy moment which stretched credulity and alienated many in the audience, Brother Duckett even went after the beloved Oak Ridge Boys and their chart topper *Elvira*. While he hadn't yet unraveled the specific hidden message in the lyrics *Giddy Up, Oom Poppa Oom Poppa Mow Mow,* he assured us he was working on it and knew it was something bad. And anyway, he said, country music was just a gateway to more habit-forming tunes.

To tell you the truth, he blurted, this country stuff is worse than rock in a lot of ways because they sing slower and you can understand the words easier.

Whatever one thought of Brother Duckett and his message, there was no denying he had a formula for revival success, and it relied heavily on the principal of attrition. However unconvincing his preaching may have been to apathetic high schoolers, his mastery shone through when the message ended and the invitation began. There, he implemented a witheringly effective scheme calculated to draw students inexorably to the altar.

The overarching strategy was to drag the invitation out interminably until the quota was reached, and he had perfected an alternating, gentle preacher—angry preacher bit to help the process along. One stanza of the invitational hymn would be accompanied by a jarring, jaw-flapping pounding of the pulpit, the next cushioned by sobbing pleas. If you weren't terrorized into going forward by the violence of the initial appeal, the pitiful wails to follow would hopefully tug at the heartstrings. Students immune to both approaches were confronted with the bleak reality that it was going to keep going, verse after verse, until they made a commitment.

---

Now it was Friday and Brother Duckett had one more shot at us. He had begun by reminding us of his last revival in Kentucky. There, he declared, the entire student body had flocked, trembling and contrite, to the altar.

He needed that to happen again and was very nearly frothing at the mouth. The final message was aimed squarely at the hardest of hardened hearts yet to walk the aisle. The pressure began to build in the auditorium as he spewed out Old Testament stories interspersed with other more contemporary accounts of tragedies visited upon those who squandered their last chance to Get Right with God by failing to get off the rock music.

It was becoming plain this final revival service was going to be unprecedented. From all sides, I sensed the beady eyes of faculty, laser-like, concentrated on those of us who had so far refused to respond. Other than Barrett, who was taking a nap, other holdouts were showing signs of nerves. I cupped a hand over my mouth and leaned toward Woody who, sensing my weakening resolve, whispered his instructions before I could ask the question.

We. Ain't. Goin. Forward.

Now the end was near. Brother Duckett was rolling, pacing authoritatively east and west across the platform, his voice booming dramatically, gesticulating wildly. King James folded over between his thumb and forefinger, he thumped it loudly on his palm. The crowd looked to be fairly softened up, so he pulled a clipping from his Bible to deliver his devastating peroration. The story involved Elvis Presley, now five years in his grave. Brother Duckett mustered his thoughts, hitched up his pants and took a deep breath, hesitating as he looked across the room to assure himself that all attention was still fixated on the platform for this, the final punch.

Grimly Brother Duckett read the article, pausing after every phrase. The substance of the report was that Elvis, following years of rebellious living and drug-snorting, had been compelled to wear diapers in his final concerts.

Think about that, young people, he said. The King of Rock and Roll, and he couldn't even control his bladder. That's where this garbage will take you.

Brother Duckett intended the tidbit to deliver colossal shock value, but it fell flat. By this point, incontinence was virtually the only remaining malady he hadn't yet linked to rock music, and it didn't seem so bad compared to some of the others.

A few titters filtered through the auditorium, and Brother Duckett wrinkled his brow, perhaps aware he had erred in his choice of anecdotes. And indeed he had. Elvis was at this point a historical footnote to most in the audience, and utterly irrelevant. More problematically, Brother Duckett had introduced the human urinary system into the thought process of several hundred junior high boys.

Sensing the crowd's attention leaking, if you will, Brother Duckett scrambled to regain control. He thumped the Bible on the pulpit again and ordered us to stand. Every eye closed, every head bowed, he shouted.

Here it comes, Woody whispered. Remember ...

The pianist began to hammer out a few chords as the preacher made his final push.

I want you to come forward, he said, now reverting to the tender, sympathetic voice. I want everyone who will make a commitment right here, right now, today, to give up rock music to come on forward.

A great mass of people—something like half the student body, even people who were only listening to John Denver—made their way to the front on the first stanza of *I Surrender All*.

Brother Duckett looked out and saw he still had work to do. No doubt he expected this and seamlessly transitioned to the next level of coercion.

Play another verse! he said to the pianist without looking her way. Once again the handkerchief came out, another river was wiped from his head, and then he snorted powerfully to clear the nasal passages.

Young people, he said, those of you who are still out there, I want you to listen to me, right now.

He tapped on the pulpit ominously.

If you won't come forward in a service like this ... I (tap) really (tap) wonder (tap) ... how you can even be saved. If you can't give up a little old thing like rock music, then I have no doubt you are in the clutches of the Evil One. Your soul hangs in the balance. For all I know, this is your last chance.

Another clump of students went forward. The ranks were thinning. Suddenly the *We Ain't Going Forward* plan was beginning to seem foolhardy. It was becoming like a perverse variation of a childhood last one out game, with the last one out going to hell, or at least being shunned.

I lifted my head briefly to see if Brother Duckett was ready to pack it in, but he was transitioning back to angry preacher mode. Don't you quench the spirit! Don't you dare quench the spirit!

Apprehension mushroomed. Sensing I was in danger of folding, Woody leaned over and said it again: We ain't going forward.

I don't know, I murmured behind my hand, seeing our entire pew had emptied. We might be the only ones left, I said.

A few more tedious verses went by. Our heads were bowed, but penetrating stares from the front were palpable. Brother Duckett was pouring it on now and there was undisguised contempt in his voice for the few malingerers who had yet to go forward.

I think we might have to go down, I said under my breath.

There was a brief pause as Woody considered the matter.

Did Barlow go? he asked.

I stole another discreet glance and there, unbelievably, making his way down the aisle was Barlow Barrett, having awakened from his nap, visibly annoyed but resigned. This had never happened. A wave of panic swept over me as I realized we appeared to be the only ones left. Brother Duckett was on the cusp of victory, and there was no way he would quit now.

We've got to go. We've got to go, I whispered urgently.

No, Woody said. We said we ain't going up, and we ain't going up.

Everybody in the whole school is watching us, I said.

Warily, Woody raised his head and saw it was true. We were the absolute center of the universe. Brother Duckett had us sighted. Teachers were boring through us with utter scorn. Even the other students congregating at the altar were looking back with disdain. They wanted it to be over.

―――

MANY THINGS about teenage boys are inexplicable and inexcusable, including that they are sometimes prone to uncontrollable fits of laughter in the most inappropriate of situations. And there is no more inappropriate moment to laugh than when several hundred people are imploring you to Get Right with God.

I felt it coming on and tried mightily to contain it. Someone had once told me your brain can only process one thought at a time so I started a chant in my head and began to repeat it as fast as I could: this is serious, don't laugh, this is serious, don't laugh, this is serious, don't laugh.

This worked until about the third recital, when suddenly an irrepressible image of an obese Elvis in the diapers popped into my head. Before I could get back to my chant he was bending over the edge of the stage with a lovely screaming girl draping a lei around his neck. All sweaty, like Brother Duckett, little flaps of the diapers sticking out of the back of his leather pants.

At this point I dropped my head and went into convulsions. And then Woody lost it too, his laughter coming on so suddenly, a string of mucus shot from his nostril and landed on the pew in front of us. We were in big, big trouble.

There was now no longer any possibility of recovery, and the only thing to do was try to disguise it. Heads down, hands covering faces, as if we were praying. Actually we were praying for help to stop laughing.

Woody choked out two words: Let's go.

With our expressions concealed, we stepped to the aisle and strode forward, trembling, tears now streaming down our faces. We could only hope we gave the appearance of two boys who were wrestling against the conviction of the Spirit.

Don't fight it young men, Brother Duckett yelled, pointing his Bible at us like a sword. Come on down. That's right. Come on down, right this instant!

It was a long way to the front, and somehow we recovered on the journey and attached ourselves to the great mass standing meekly below the platform. From this vantage point, Brother Duckett towered above us all, larger than life.

He made one more sweep of the handkerchief. Then he looked out wonderingly on the deserted pews. As he turned away from the pulpit, his conquest complete, he closed his immense Bible and tucked it under his arm. I thought I saw a smile emerging on his lips as he walked away.

## Chapter 17

## *Frank Woodfin and the Big Red Truck*

I was stunned to get the news that Frank Woodfin had toppled over dead without any warning whatsoever, but the moment I heard about it I could only think of that little four-word command of doom.

EVERYBODY ON THE LINE.

It meant suffering was eminent.

Everybody would get on the line. Coach Bindler would grab a stack of orange cones and go trotting up the field, laying one out every so often. He would set a cone down, then run out ten or fifteen or twenty yards further and set another one down.

Some days he went almost out to the railroad tracks, fading to an apparition in the heat shimmer, depositing those funnels of misery all the way. The whistle blew, and we sprinted to the first cone, sprinted back to the line, sprinted to the second cone, sprinted back, sprinted to the third cone, et cetera, ad nauseam, excrucio. If at any time he felt anyone wasn't going all out he would add more cones and yell EVERYBODY ON THE LINE again, and we would start over. Some people called them suicide sprints. Homicide sprints was more like it.

Coach did not like to make cuts. He preferred that people quit. Drop On Request. I want your D.O.R. He loved to make it happen. Nobody died, but I don't know how.

If you wanted to play soccer at Temple High you needed more than skills. You had to survive EVERYBODY ON THE LINE and an assortment of other unsophisticated cruelties.

A lot of people didn't make it past the first smoldering August day two weeks before school started. The proceedings began back at the gym with the obligatory but spectacularly superficial sports physical, conducted by a scruffy old gentleman purporting to be a medical doctor who charged five dollars per athlete.

He completed thirty physicals in about twenty minutes.

Three step examination, it was. First, he laid a stethoscope on the chest momentarily, perhaps long enough to confirm a single heartbeat. Next the patient was ordered to drop his jock, whereupon the scrotum was poked with what seemed like excessive violence. Finally, he invested a nanosecond or two performing a visual body scan. Absent anything glaring—like a missing limb or end-stage elephantiasis—the man would wave you through and grunt for the next patient. No one ever failed.

Then it was on to the practice field. Except the field was nowhere in the vicinity, and it really wasn't a field. It was a wretched piece of real estate a mile away, off Watkins Street. More of a landfill to be honest, riddled as it was with discarded beer cans, mutant weeds, broken glass, cigarette butts, ruts, dog excrement—hopefully it was dog—and gopher holes just waiting to liquefy ankle ligaments. The air thick with nostril-burning industrial odors wafting over from nearby plants. The field was owned by an adjacent factory, whose owners allowed the team its use for free when they didn't need it for parking semi-trailers.

Every day we made the gallop from campus through drug-infested neighborhoods to begin three hours of sit ups, push-ups, leg lifts, and a punishing potpourri of running drills, always culminating with the fearful EVERYBODY ON THE LINE.

And Coach Bindler didn't spend any time worrying about hydration. There were days when no water was brought to the field at all, and when it was available access was highly restricted. Fluid deprivation was considered part of the process needed to instill toughness and cull the weaklings.

Thirst and pain were assured, as was the appearance of a certain diminutive visitor. At some point during every practice, every day, a big red Ford pickup truck whisked into the adjacent lot, stirring up a cloud of gravel dust. The driver's door would swing open, and out would step Frank Woodfin, pride of Dade County, Georgia. He would make a subtle little three-fingered adjustment to his ball cap—also red most of the time—amble up to the hood, and watch from a distance.

Mr. Woodfin was a coach, though not of this team. He came as an observer.

---

CK Supply over on Main Street, that's where he worked. It was a dilapidated building partially visible from the field, mostly obscured by an impenetrable stand of kudzu. I was never entirely sure what Mr. Woodfin did there. Sheetrock sales, or something. Whatever it was, he didn't let it get in the way of making a daily appearance at practice.

His son Woody became my best friend. We were connected by the misery shared out on Watkins field. Woody was a fine athlete, though not the biggest or fastest or most skilled. What he had, in abundance, was heart. Always the first one to the line, and always the only player who refused to collapse to the ground or double over at the finish. Woody stood straight while the rest of us bent, choking and gasping.

I tried to stand straight, too. Couldn't do it. I'd like to say it was the asthma—a lifelong struggle—worsened by those noxious factory fumes and the kiln heat of summer in the south. Deep down inside, though, I always knew my lungs were big enough but my heart wasn't.

One day after a summer morning practice Woody suggested we walk down to Armando's for lunch.

My dad's over there, said Woody.

How do you know that?

Because he's there every day.

Armando's was the prototypical neighborhood burger joint. Hole in the wall. The entire menu fit on one side of one sheet of paper. Not a big sheet of paper like at those fine dining places, but a little slip, like church bulletin size.

The red truck was there, sure enough.

We walked in and were waved over by Mr. Woodfin at his booth where he was presiding over his standard fare of cheeseburger, fries and Sprite. He adjusted his cap with the three fingers and said, How's practice, boys?

Terrible, I said.

Terrible, Woody said.

I'm about ready to quit, I offered. Coach Bindler's trying to kill us, and all that stuff from the factories is getting in my lungs, and I have asthma real bad.

You ain't gonna quit, said Mr. Woodfin. You ain't ever gonna quit.

Mr. Woodfin didn't appear to have heard the part about the asthma, or he ignored it. He had become unsettled by the word *quit*, which he didn't care for.

There wasn't any animus in the way he responded. Kindly,

really, with a hint of a wry smile, and his voice lacked resonance. But somehow it seemed authoritative.

Ya'll boys want a cheeseburger? he asked.

Yes Sir, Woody said.

Yes Sir, I said.

The lunch was free, but it wasn't. The thing about real coaches is they never miss an opportunity to coach, even in Armando's.

Now listen here, Mr. Woodfin said. The one thing you got to have on that ball field is character. That means you ain't ever going to quit. God might give somebody else more skill, but hustle is up to you. There's no reason to be outhustled by anyone, ever.

Little cap adjustment, again. Sip of sprite. Continue.

The good Lord gives you an opportunity, you take it. Don't squander any opportunity. Not everybody gets to play ball. And you won't, for very long. You got to do your best, and you ain't ever gonna quit. Right?

Yes Sir, I said.

Yes Sir, Woody said.

I listened, because the man had a track record of turning middling ball players into champions. Everybody in Dade County and plenty of people elsewhere knew about Coach Woodfin and his underdog, underdogged, overachiever little league teams. He was genius camouflaged in rustic. His words were sparse but measured and calculated to motivate and capable of coaxing talent out of hopeless cases.

---

THERE WAS THIS SEASON-ENDING PARTY, later, and the soccer team went for bowling and pizza. The team manager, Jeremy, was trying to bowl. This kid, who was closely modeled after the Gilligan character of the Island, was manager of the team because he had no hope of playing. He had the coordination of gelatin and had gone through the season serving primarily as the target for every practical joke imaginable, most of them involving underwear—his or others'—being stretched to epic proportions and eventually becoming affixed in some manner to the poor boy's head.

At the bowling alley he was zero for six frames and drawing more abuse, having deposited each of his efforts directly into the gutter. When one of his oafishly tossed balls somehow stayed in the lane—albeit moving slowly—someone pushed the reset button to bring the bar down and block his effort. Jeremy then was forced to walk down the lane to retrieve his stalled ball, which brought the alley manager out of his booth with a scathing castigation.

Great fun, it was, and everybody had another good laugh at Jeremy.

Later I looked over, and there was Mr. Woodfin coaching Jeremy. I didn't hear what was said but could tell from the motions he was talking to him about positioning, and footwork, and aligning his shoulder this way and his hips that way.

Waste of time, I thought. But a few minutes later Jeremy was rolling the ball down the middle of the lane. Unbelievable. Nobody would have ever thought to coach the team manager or supposed it would do any good if they did, except for Mr. Woodfin. He had the kid chock full of confidence, at least until his next wedgie.

―――

We walked out of Armando's back into the sun. Mr. Woodfin gave us a ride back to the gym.

Ya'll be good, he said.

Yes Sir.

Yes Sir.

I wasn't really going to quit, I said as we got out.

I know, he said.

The red truck trailed away.

One thing, Woody said. Don't ever say nothing about quitting to my dad. Drives him crazy. It don't matter if you're any good or not, because he can make you better. The only thing he don't like is quitting.

———

That big red Ford truck, it went all over Tennessee, with Frank Woodfin and his little wife Melba, who was always scooted up next to him close like they were teenagers. Every soccer game, every basketball game, every baseball game. Home and away. Regular season, tournaments, playoffs. If the school bus was going to a game, the big red truck was behind it. Weekday, weekend, immaterial. Distance, irrelevant.

He probably lost some sheetrock sales, or whatever.

And now and then we'd be standing out by the truck after the game or maybe sitting in McDonalds and Mr. Woodfin would adjust his ballcap and say, in his subtle and understated way, you might had done this or done that, or pressed forward at this point or crossed this ball earlier or pushed up the right wing because their left back has no speed, and when we play them at our place next month remember to keep that forward on his weaker foot and he won't be able to do a thing.

He would see stuff you would never see on your own, and suddenly a light bulb would click on in your head and you would realize the man had an understanding about things that could sharpen your game, give you an edge.

But none of it did any good unless you could survive

EVERYBODY ON THE LINE, back at Watkins Field. It was a dump by anyone's definition to be sure, but it was also an incubator of dreams.

———

ALL THESE YEARS later I heard EVERYBODY ON THE LINE again in my head, as the jet forged its way across America in the night, with me inside on my way to the funeral of Frank Woodfin. After four sleepless hours the lights of Atlanta fluttered on the horizon, then gathered and brightened, and in a few moments more we glided down from the blackness. I shouldered a bag, trekked through a desolate terminal, and boarded a shuttle bus for the long ride home. We merged onto Interstate 75 and Olympic Stadium came into view, its torch blazing high above the grandstands. A few nights earlier I had watched from my living room as a trembling Muhammad Ali had applied the flame to open the 1996 ceremonies.

Frank Woodfin had seen that very flame just the other day. But now his heart had quit on him, the only part of him that ever did.

At New Salem Baptist up on Lookout Mountain, the front door was wedged tight with a bigger crowd of people than the architect ever contemplated. In this same church Frank Woodfin had been enjoying last Sunday morning's preaching. Had just belted out a hearty Amen when he went down. Fifty-seven years old, and probably dead before he hit the floor, the doctor said.

Someone motioned for me to sit with the family, so I shuffled in with them through a side door to the three or four rows reserved up front. The pews filled quietly behind me with what looked like every person the man had ever coached. Standing room only, and then the standing room was filled.

Seemed like a lot of people for a sheetrock salesman, or whatever.

We got the funeral over with and everyone went over to the fellowship hall for the meal which involved a stupendous quantity of food, and an endless parade of former ball players who wanted to say how Frank Woodfin had made them better, talked about opportunity, taught them they could do anything, as long as they didn't quit.

———

It didn't seem right that he would be gone and I wondered, what would Frank Woodfin have done with the final stanza of his life, had he known it was such? What would he have done, say, with the last three days God gave him?

I could guess.

I could guess he would take one of those days to relish with his three children. Taking in a baseball game like they had done so many times before, being sure to tell them—not together, but one by one—how much he loved them. And maybe he'd spend a morning with his best buddies on the golf course, savoring one last outing with them. With any luck he'd hit the ball on the screws and split the fairway and make the little three-fingered adjustment to his ball cap and do it again on the next tee, and the one after that too. Perhaps it would be his finest round of the year.

And I could guess he surely would take a day just to be with his wife, who even after all these years never did get comfortable sitting way over on the passenger's side.

I could guess, but I didn't have to.

Because the things Frank Woodfin would have done are precisely the things he did do.

Even though by anyone's guess—his included, surely—he had more decades of life to enjoy.

---

I AM on the return redeye, flying back home to Arizona.

Everyone in the cabin but me is sleeping. I close my eyes and I see him. He's in the casket, but that's not really him, and the image of the deceased Frank Woodfin from today isn't nearly as powerful as the alive Frank Woodfin from long ago. There he is as I look out the back of the school bus, following in the red truck with Melba, driving all over Tennessee.

And there he is, sitting across from me in Armando's, and—

I am hunched over, hands on my knees, wheezing for breath, every muscle burning. My mouth is a paste factory, and someone has reached down and ripped the lungs out of my chest. The air is ovenesque and it tastes like chemicals and dog crap. Coach Bindler, that maniac, is out there laying more cones. Can we get some water? somebody asks. Bindler says no, maybe later, if I see the kind of effort I want to see. A voice inside me says you can't do this. You have asthma. It's not worth it. You can't.

From the corner of my eye, I see a crimson image arcing into the gravel lot, a rooster tail of dust kicking up behind. It's the big red truck, grinding to a stop, the cloud overtaking it for a moment and then floating away, dissipating. I look up and see the form of a slender man climb out. He stands by the hood, he puts on his ball cap, makes his three-fingered adjustment, he watches from a distance.

EVERYBODY ON THE LINE, the coach yells for the millionth time.

I stand up straight.

And I say to myself, no way am I quitting today.

# Chapter 18

## *We Know Who You Are*

SITTING ALL DAY ON AN UNPADDED HARDWOOD PEW AS THE feeling inevitably went out of your buttocks was a situation crying out for diversion. Luckily there was the giant death clock. And Dr. Clyde's announcements.

Temple Academy was just the sidekick of a much larger institution, namely Tennessee Temple University. They shared the campus and the dogma, and once a year the high school students were required to attend the University's missionary conference, which was only marginally less painful than the detention experience.

I normally liked missionaries and enjoyed hearing their stories about faraway lands and jungles and narrow escapes from death. But the University eggheads contrived to make the conference appallingly boring. They stocked the speaking schedule with enfeebled white-haired bureaucrats from missionary agencies who'd left the actual mission fields decades earlier—if they'd been at all—and their messages were dry and dull.

Each day the conference began at eight thirty in the

morning and continued all day, with one excruciating speaker after another until the school day ended.

Then there were the evening sessions.

And you had to be careful, because the University had a supercharged henchman by the name of Dr. Clyde Bennington who was infinitely more fearsome than the high school's Dr. Winters. The mere sight of him surveilling students froze the blood.

Dr. Bennington was a juggernaut of a man, a towering, barrel-chested tyrant who ruled the campus with unflinching authority. He was patently humorless and suffered no fools or folly. *Dean of Students* was the title, but that label failed to convey the power he wielded and the terror he instilled. With a wave of the finger Dr. Clyde could command your expulsion for the slightest offense. If you had the misfortune of passing over the threshold of his office, you were traveling beyond the realm of mercy.

There was a well-established protocol at the University for processing people who were Not Right with God. Depending on the offense or the number of times you had offended, you could be summoned to see the President, the Chancellor, or the Dean of Students. The President and the Chancellor were, on the surface, kindly gentlemen known to offer second chances. If your appointment was with one of those two you had a shot of continuing your academic career, provided you showed an extreme level of humility and repentance.

But if beckoned into Dr. Clyde's office there was only one possible outcome. I had observed many shattered college students—grown men and women—crying like babies as they sat trembling in the glass-enclosed waiting room for their terminal visit with the Dean.

By all appearances he was a robot. Rarely seen outside of church and chapel services, Dr. Clyde was a reliable fixture on the platform of every conference session, where he would sit Stalinesque and stoic, ramrod straight and unmoving, gimlet eyes hidden behind a monstrous pair of Coke bottle glasses. The stillness was an illusion, though, because he was feverishly at work every moment. Behind those spectacles he was systematically scanning three thousand seats across two levels for anyone who might be showing indications of being Not Right with God.

It was almost supernatural, the way he patrolled that room. It wasn't a normal auditorium, having been expanded in fits and starts over the years to accommodate an ever-growing body of students. Walls had been knocked out at odd angles, balconies expanded, and pockets of pews wedged into every nook and cranny, leaving all manner of weird angles and obstructed sight lines.

Naïve freshman seeking alternate entertainment during a service would often scout a spot where it seemed certain they were out of view of Dr. Clyde. Feeling isolated and comfortable, they would begin their activities, which ran the gamut from engaging in inappropriate physical contact to playing Electronic Quarterback.

Mystically Dr. Clyde would vanish from the platform and materialize almost instantly in the vicinity of the reprobates. A spindly finger would motion the guilty from the pew, names would be recorded, and appointments scheduled.

---

Dr. Clyde's sole official duty during the service was to read the announcements, and even in this he imparted fear. The vast frame looming over the pulpit, the brooding expression, and the booming voice all led a menacing quality to the birthday greetings, prayer requests, event notices, and reminders about behavioral expectations. Whenever he mentioned a rule, you knew it was because he had just expelled a student for violation of said rule. He might say, for example: I want to remind students that attendance at all Sunday evening services is mandatory. You cannot attend Tennessee Temple and choose not to attend Sunday evening church.

If he made that announcement, you knew some poor soul had just been apprehended emerging from a nearby movie theater having elected to take in *Porky's II* instead of the evening service. And, following a visit to Dr. Clyde's office, was now packing his bags. Campus security officers in mufti doubled as secret police for the Dean. He regularly dispatched them to known hangouts where they would spot and report students who were at the wrong place at the wrong time.

The greatest element of intrigue with Dr. Clyde was when he would announce that some illicit act had occurred and demand that the guilty parties come forward to confess.

*We Know Who You Are*, he would say, with the implication they might get a shred of grace if they confessed voluntarily.

Thing is, you never really could tell if he really did Know Who You Are.

Perhaps he really did know, and the announcement was a veiled opportunity for the offenders to escape with probation ... provided they came clean before receiving the dreaded summons.

Or, Dr. Clyde might not really have the slightest clue who was responsible for installing the Mickey Mouse hands on the church clock, and the announcement was a subterfuge calculated to ferret out the criminals so they could be expelled forthwith.

The sensible thing to do for anyone looking for a bit of fun would be to stay as far away from Dr. Clyde as humanly possible. But young people often insist on getting their kicks by going right into the mouth of the lion.

Dr. Clyde was about to become a caricature of himself with the weak spot proving to be, surprisingly, the daily announcements read from the pulpit. His handicap was that he—along with everyone else in the administration—was entirely detached from popular culture in general and rock music in particular.

It started on the first day of the missionary conference. Dr. Clyde had shuffled through several index cards in his stack of messages when he announced:

We want to wish a happy birthday today to Jethro Tull.

As the crowed disintegrated, Doctor Clyde was frozen for a moment, and then his expressionless face became a great sheet of crimson. He waited for the laughter to die down, which took a long time.

I want to remind students, he said gravely, that this is not a time or place for jokes. Those who submit inappropriate announcements will be dealt with severely. We know who you are.

But in this case Dr. Clyde clearly didn't know who the perpetrators were because the Jethro Tull prank spawned a raft of bogus announcements which multiplied as the week went on. Tuesday brought a special welcome to prospective student Bill Joel who was visiting from Allentown, and a request for Ric Ocasek to move his car which was said to be parked in a handicap zone. On Wednesday, he invited those interested in mission work with refugees to meet Brother Tom Petty in the lobby after the service. As soon as the guffaws subsided on that one, he innocently offered up a prayer request for Rupert Holmes.

The genius of it was there was no practical way to avoid the bogus announcements, because doing so would require Dr.

Clyde to acquaint himself with the rock music industry and its' artists, and that simply wasn't going to happen. It would be akin to him being in possession of the names of all the performers at the gentleman's club on Market Street. Questions would be raised as to how he had acquired the information. Brother Duckett, the high school revivalist, might have had a special dispensation to delve into the dark world of rock music, but Dr. Clyde didn't.

By Thursday, the situation had become untenable for Dr. Clyde, given that snickers were rippling through the auditorium even before he'd approached the pulpit. Nobody had ever laughed at him before, at least not in his presence.

This time he skipped the announcements altogether and instead delivered a thunderous attack on those who would befoul the proceedings with such chicanery.

Those of you who have chosen to make a mockery of this conference, he said, would be wise to confess your sins before the day is out and ask forgiveness, and Get Right with God. In any event, we know who you are.

He glared out across the auditorium and continued.

Moreover, we've instituted a new procedure, beginning today. All announcements must be brought to my office prior to the service. They will be screened beforehand. Any announcement that has not been screened and approved in advance will not be made.

Dr. Clyde then went on to reiterate that the people submitting the false announcements were in danger of being called home to glory, or wherever they were going, because they were undoubtedly of no further use to God. And, he added, expulsion was the least of their worries.

His solution to the problem, it would emerge, was the employment of a seminary student, freshly enrolled and new to the faith, to vet the announcements. As a recent convert, the young man could admit familiarity with the rock music industry without incriminating himself.

---

MESSING about with Doctor Clyde was one thing, but a more sustained diversion was provided by the gigantic, electronic death clock bolted to the wall above the speakers' platform. Larger than a basketball scoreboard, the death clock was designed to provide a continual, sobering reminder to the audience of how fast people were dying without Jesus. But sadly, in short order it was reduced to an instrument of low-grade entertainment and medium stakes wagering.

The death clock tallied the rate at which people were expiring all over the world. It started on Monday morning at zero and ran all week. The intent, ostensibly, was to spur attendees to greater urgency in their evangelistic endeavors.

The problem was that the clock moved so fast it evoked a sense of abject hopelessness and futility, and lost its ability to shock after about five minutes. Something like two people die on the planet every second, which meant that we lost 400 souls just while singing Bringing in the Sheaves. Like a child opening a lemonade stand to help pay off the national debt, the numbers quickly proved too formidable to elicit the desired feeling of empathy.

At first you would look at the numbers as they climbed at breakneck speed and think about how awful it was, all those people dying so quickly. It was only natural, next, to visualize how they might be expiring, and a panoply of grisly accidents and ghastly diseases rolled through your mind. But the human brain only allows such thoughts to linger for a short time. After a while you would realize you were just watching the death clock compute without quite feeling any sense of horror.

And then it would dawn on you. As monotonous as the death clock might be, it was still a lot more interesting than the speaker, who was deep into an exposition of Obadiah or some other obscure passage. And, inevitably, the next logical thought would be to begin making calculations on how many people would kick the bucket by the time the sermon ended.

From there it was only a short hop to bookmaking. By the second day of the conference, a list made its way down the pew. Students wrote their name, and next to it a number representing their projection of the death clock tally at the moment the sermon ended. Soon the exercise involved gambling. Your wager was more than merely a mathematical exercise because speakers rarely ended their sermons at the designated time. To have a realistic shot at the pool, you had to have some knowledge of the particular speaker's penchant for long-windedness.

During one service Dr. Clyde materialized from nowhere and confiscated the betting sheet as it reached the end of the row. However he wasn't able to decipher the data and probably assumed it was some kind of Bible code, so we escaped prosecution. His greatest moment of consternation came when the death clock rolled over to one million on the final day of the conference, right in the middle of an especially dry sermon by the Reverend Lehmann Strauss, and a contingent of students began applauding.

Dr. Clyde had been terrifying and invincible for decades and no one thought he could ever be toppled, but something had gone out of him with the bogus chapel announcements. In later months he became the object of pranks that grew in their audacity and sophistication including, incredibly, the late-night installation of a Volkswagen Beetle, sans wheels, in his office foyer.

It all ended when a rival in the administration—a man with designs on his Dean of Students position—discovered that Dr.

Clyde was himself engaged in an inappropriate relationship with a staff member. The rival arranged to have the lines tapped and suddenly, Dr. Clyde was quietly and quickly sent away, just as he had done to so many others.

In the years following, the administration took pains to scrutinize announcements, but sometimes one would slip through, and we would be reminded of the reign of Dr. Clyde.

I saw him once, years later, in the grocery store. He looked my way, but blankly. I felt that twinge of fear, but then realized all the formidability had been drawn out of him. He was just a frail old man picking up some bread.

I know who you are, I thought to myself.

## Chapter 19

## *The Whoppers*

I NEED TO APOLOGIZE TO COACH WADLEY ABOUT THE Whoppers.

Of course he would have no idea what I'm talking about. He does not remember the Whoppers. But I have never forgotten. Lord knows I've tried, but can't.

I cannot go to a store without remembering the Whoppers because they are in the checkout lane. And in every gas station. For sure, *pay at the pump* gas stations have been a welcome innovation, but every so often, the pump fails to print out my receipt, or I need something to drink, and I go into the store. And there they are, usually right under the counter, under my nose, demanding this confession.

One time I was paying at the pump and while my gas was pumping, I decided to clean my windshield. Then I forgot the gas nozzle was still in the truck and drove off. There was a big clunk as I pulled away, and I looked back to see I was towing the nozzle and about twenty feet of hose out onto the street with me. I had to go inside and report to the attendant, with no small level of mortification, that I had just destroyed his gas pump. I will never forget the expression on his face. It was not a pleasant one. I also couldn't help but notice he was standing directly above a whole row of Whoppers.

They even started selling them in cardboard cartons, the kind they put milk in. Who puts candy in a milk carton, and why? The Whoppers people do, and I know why. Because God made them do it. Sure, they think they have their reasons. They have their marketing department, and their focus groups, and a slew of scientific studies indicating that selling Whoppers in a milk carton would be a stroke of genius. But I have a suspicion it was God. Part of His plan. My sin is ever before me, wrote the psalmist, though he probably didn't realize God was having him write that for me.

I could have paid up a long time ago. I should have. I don't know why I didn't. I thought the guilt would just fade away. It's not like eating the Whoppers would make my top ten list of transgressions. But for some reason I've never been able to shake the memory. So here I am, almost forty years later, writing about the Whoppers.

I never even really liked Whoppers.

It all started with one of those school fundraisers, the ones where students go out and badger relatives and neighbors to buy something they don't want at a grotesquely inflated price. The Whoppers were for the baseball team, to help pay for equipment and the cost of road trips.

In all fairness, I believe it was not the best decision to give us the sixty boxes of Whoppers before we had sold them. These days, they've smartened up and make you collect the money before they deliver the candy, or cookies, or whatever.

I did not even personally know sixty people, so the chance of me selling all those Whoppers was somewhat remote to begin with. My intentions were good, however. I was confident in my sales acumen.

I racked up two sales the first day. Mom and Dad agreed to each purchase a box of whoppers as a philanthropic gesture, even though they were counting calories.

Thank you, that will be two dollars, I said.

Where are the Whoppers? Dad asked.

Left them at school. I will bring them home tomorrow.

OK, said my dad. The slightest of furrows materialized on his brow, suggesting he might have concerns about my ability to deliver on the agreement.

Bring us the Whoppers, he said, and we will give you the two dollars.

The next morning I was late out of bed and missed breakfast. I barely made it to my locker to retrieve my first period textbook. As it happened, my locker was the depository for the Whoppers. I grabbed a box and made myself a mental IOU.

After lunch—another box to boost my energy for afternoon classes. And Woody asked for a box. What kind of friend would deny anyone a box of Whoppers? Not me.

After school, it seemed only just to reward myself for having successfully completed the day.

The same sequence of events was repeated the next day, except this time Woody said he needed two boxes because he was trying to make a move on a girl who liked Whoppers.

Two days. Nine boxes of Whoppers down. Funds collected, zero.

Mom and Dad took delivery of their order, and I put their two dollars in an envelope with the word *Whoppers* neatly printed on the front. Early the next morning, I found I did not have sufficient fuel in my tank to reach school. I retrieved the two dollars from the envelope at the Exxon station and in short order it was vaporized through the exhaust pipe of my 1969 Buick Skylark.

I leaned on ESJ for a purchase. How much are they? she asked.

Just one dollar a box.

You're insane, she said. But give me five boxes and I will try to sell them for you.

Not only have I yet to receive any funds from this consignment arrangement, ESJ later denied the conversation ever happened, and claimed to have no memory of taking possession of any Whoppers.

Within a couple more days, almost miraculously, thirty boxes of Whoppers had vanished. Net revenue, zero.

At baseball practice, Coach Wadley asked for an accounting.

About half of my order is gone, I said.

Where's the money? he asked.

I don't have it with me, I answered.

Technically, correct.

I began to run the calculations on how I could earn the money to pay for the misappropriated Whoppers. At this time I was employed as a night janitor at the Dillard Smith Construction Company where I was paid the sum of three dollars and thirty-five cents an hour. The job mostly involved mopping floors and cleaning toilets, where I found out that construction workers are among the most wildly inaccurate urinators on the planet.

There were twenty-four toilets on the premises, and I was expected to complete the work in ninety minutes. After taxes, this worked out to about four dollars per shift, then another dollar needed to be subtracted for the cost of gasoline. If you want to look up miles per gallon on a 1969 Skylark, be my guest. It's not good.

Works out to eight toilets cleaned per box of Whoppers, with no money left for anything else.

I did not find this stark analysis to be encouraging. And you know what you do when you become discouraged and there are Whoppers within reach?

---

There comes a point in time when you realize the math is inexorably against you, and for me that point was when my inventory fell to twenty boxes. The only solution was to effectively go into hiding. I didn't exactly resign my position as manager of the baseball team, I just stopped showing up. And took elaborate diversions to avoid Coach Wadley.

Several times he cornered me in the hallway. Where is the Whopper money? Where are the Whoppers? I want the money you owe me, or I want the Whoppers back. One or the other. Or else.

Working on it, I said.

Not correct, technically. The Whoppers were gone. Like a man on death row, I had polished off the final twenty boxes in two days. And there was no money.

After I walked across the platform to graduate, I expected to open my folder and find a demand for the Whoppers money instead of a diploma. Somehow, I slipped through the cracks.

But all these years later, I hear the cry for justice. Can a man ever really Get Right with God when he's never made good on the Whoppers?

In the decades I spent pondering this, the school shut down, so this is now difficult to rectify.

All those sermons I heard about the Lamb's Book of Life in Revelation. It's supposed to be a list of everyone who is saved. At the end of time, I'm going to be standing there and Jesus is going to open that book and there'll be a sticky note in there about the Whoppers, I just know it.

## Chapter 20

## *The Church of Your Choice*

AT THE TIME I SUBMITTED MY APPLICATION FOR employment with Red Food Store #100, I was not aware it was the official dumping ground for the ineptest managers in the grocery chain. But it didn't take long to find out.

For anyone aspiring to an exciting career in the grocery store industry, there was only one real possibility in Chattanooga. The fifty-plus store Red Food chain subjugated the entire tristate grocery market and viciously destroyed all competitors. No one else had a prayer. Red Food had begun as a small, locally owned grocer at the turn of the century and its customers were fiercely loyal. Never mind that Red Food was now actually owned by a French conglomerate—a carefully concealed corporate factoid—Chattanoogans loved Red Food.

Winn Dixie? Piggly Wiggly? Food Lion? Kroger? Don't make me laugh. Red Food squashed them all like bugs. The competition vainly tried everything—double coupons, triple coupons, massive loss-leading sales—to lure customers away from the home-town stores with the hustling bag boys adorned in trademark white shirts and red clip-on bow ties. Even Red

Food's torturous, cornball commercials suggested they really didn't have any competition. Though they scarcely needed it, Red Food ran a decades-long advertising campaign that burned an annoying jingle into the psyche of the community. The powerful and profound lyrics, in their entirety, were:

*We're more than a store*
*We're more than a store*
*We're more than a store*
*We're Red Food!*

Not long after beginning my career at Red Food, it became clear to me that it was, indeed, more than a store. It was an asylum. At least, Store #100 was.

It started out well enough. I apparently dazzled in my employment interview to the extent they decided to put me in the produce department—a modest step above the lowly bag boy. Produce clerks wore a green bow tie, which was marginally more credible. Prestige is probably not the right word, but it was slightly less humiliating than running around parking lots sweating in a red bow tie. I would be working intimately with the fruits and vegetables and would avoid the harsh elements. I did not, to be candid, know a lot about produce and my exposure to fruit generally came in the form of Pop Tarts. But I was eager to learn. And as the owner of the ancient and unwieldy gas-sucking Buick, I was willing to do whatever it took to earn money for transportation and dates.

The general public—and uninitiated new employees like me—knew Red Food #100 simply as the downtown store on Ninth Street. But every veteran Red Food manager knew something ominous about Store #100—the mere mention of it conjured up the stench of career death. It was, in fact, the graveyard of Red Foods, a place from which there was no return, professionally speaking. It was to be avoided at any cost.

The way it worked in management at Red Food was that if

you did not meet corporate's expectations, you would simply be fired. But if you had some annoying trait, or did something really, really despicable or exceptionally dumb—and firing was not deemed to be sufficient punishment—you would be sent to manage Red Food #100. The end result was ultimately the same, career-wise, but the downtown store served as a form of purgatory where you could be put through a regimen of intense suffering until your management career came to an ignominious end.

It was absolutely impossible to successfully manage Store #100 because it attracted the perfect storm of the most implacable customers imaginable.

First, it was planted adjacent to a high-crime area and its principal customers were experts in the five-finger discount. An unrelenting epidemic of shoplifting erased any chance of profitability from the start. Second, the store sat at the foot of Cameron Hill, a high dollar luxury condo complex where many of the city's wealthy lived. These citizens demanded a level of service and exotic food choices that Red Food was unwilling and unable to offer. They were hateful and scornful, and looked upon you—on being told that Red Food did not carry Wasabi root, for example—with intense disdain. And third, #100 was the only grocery store in range of the Jaycee Towers, an assisted-living center for cantankerous seniors who —drawing upon thousands of years of collective experience— had become professional complainants. They protested virtually everything, were utterly unappeasable, and often took their grievances straight to the top.

I happened to begin my career at Red Food at about the same time that Mr. Dwight P. Crumpler was transferred to Store #100 as the new manager. It was not difficult to ascertain what had caused Crumpler to earn his punitive assignment. He had several glaring quirks, but the most annoying, by far, was his over the top optimism.

Mr. Crumpler, a counterpart to the Super Mario character of Nintendo fame, was a beefy, mustachioed fellow who waddled around frantically shouting encouragement to employees and aggressively greeting every customer, whether they wanted it or not. And because Crumpler suffered from some hearing loss, everything he conveyed was delivered at a tremendous volume.

He had attended some sort of motivational seminar at which he was, I guess, instructed to be happy and affirming. But Crumpler had taken the concept to extreme levels. It was like the power of positive thinking on anabolic steroids. Even Norman Vincent Peale, I suspect, would have found him to be insufferable. When his enthusiasm rubbed someone at corporate the wrong way and he found himself at the helm of Store #100, Crumpler inexplicably embraced it as good news. The demotion, in effect, meant he was only ever going to leave this Red Food via termination, retirement, or a pine box, and yet deep down inside he must have believed he could beat the rap. At all hours of the day and night he was vehemently cheerful to employees, supervisors, customers and vendors, and it seemed no amount of bad news could dampen his mood.

Not being the most nuanced individual, Crumpler's optimism played out in a singular fashion with the repetitive and gymnastic use of the word GREAT! He didn't just say it, but added a feral quality to it, like Tony the Tiger, bellowing the exclamation from the depths of his lungs, every time. It didn't matter what was being discussed, he worked it into every conversation, as if the word held some magical quality that would increase exponentially the louder he said it.

Good morning, Mr. Crumpler, I would say upon arrival.

GREAT MORNING TO YOU! he would retaliate, as I

resisted the instinct to shield my eardrums. AND IT'S A GREAT DAY TO BE WORKING AT RED FOOD! On the far side of the store, people shopping in the bread aisle would wince.

Pedro Riggins, manager of the produce department, had a much different deficiency. He was knowledgeable about the fruits and vegetables and was a capable administrator, but his disqualifying flaw was that he would cry whenever reprimanded—which was often. Pedro was terrified of upper management, and as soon as the yelling started, the tears would flow uncontrollably.

I felt bad for Pedro. His insecurities likely stemmed from the name. He was from moonshine country deep in the hills of Tennessee, and neither he nor anyone within miles of his home had any trace of Spanish lineage. Why his parents saddled him with the name Pedro was never satisfactorily explained to him, but he once speculated they must have been on a bender when they made the selection. All he knew for sure was that it was the cause of all manner of abuse in his formative years.

At regular intervals a bantamweight district manager with a Napoleonic complex named Max Wickham would arrive and summon Pedro to the back room, where he would be informed that his department was the worst produce operation in the history of Red Food. Wickham, who did not share Crumpler's positive reinforcement philosophy, would scream and rant until the waterworks started.

He doubtless did not get this type of rewarding response from other managers, and Wickham surely relished in the spectacle of reducing Pedro's emotions to romper room status. As time went by it seemed his visits became more frequent and I sensed he was simply entertaining himself.

I think I'll stop by Store #100 on my way home and make Pedro cry again, I presume was his thinking.

Finally, and most remarkably, there was Mr. Ernie Pawlak, the assistant manager. Like Crumpler he was enthusiastic, but his fervor showed in a more militaristic style. Pawlak had gone to Tennessee Temple with an eye on training for the ministry but had never made it past the first year. He once told me that after entering college, he had realized the Lord had not called him to preach, but to instead work at Red Food. Based on a raft of similar stories with which I was familiar, I took this to mean he had either run out of tuition money or impregnated his girlfriend, but he never let on which it was.

Pawlak was a wiry guy with a scraggy mustache and a penchant for Old Spice aftershave, the scent of which preceded him as he patrolled the store. Red Food was now Pawlak's life's mission, and he took to it with evangelistic zeal. He literally ran from point to point, covering untold miles with every shift, and expected everyone else to do the same.

His specialty was procuring free labor for Red Food. Pawlak had developed several techniques that became the bane of every bag boy. The store paid its employees in quarter-hour increments, and Pawlak had reckoned that if workers clocked in seven minutes before their shift started, and clocked out seven minutes after it ended, he could get an extra fourteen minutes of work daily without paying for it. Moreover, he would assign tasks to employees immediately after they had clocked out to get just a little more. High-strung and neurotic, Pawlak became obsessed with this strategy and eventually took to clocking people out himself at seven minutes after the hour, without their knowledge.

But Pawlak rose to his greatest heights whenever a potential shoplifter entered the store. He fancied himself as a one-man shrinkage prevention machine and had an instinct for sniffing out thieves. He stalked suspects from hidden corners and regularly chased robbers for blocks with complete disregard for the possibility they might be armed, which they often were.

Every time he recovered Red Food merchandise without getting shot or sliced up, Pawlak saw it as reaffirmation that God had called him for this. And as his bravura expanded, he took to dangling a set of handcuffs from his belt loop, both as a warning to prospective lawbreakers and as an aid in making citizen's arrests.

Yet once Pawlak had a crook cornered or in custody, he transformed into a pacifist, convinced he could be an agent of transformation. And here, he deviated significantly from the Red Food management policy manual by offering to waive charges if the offender simply agreed to attend church on the upcoming Sunday. The terms of the bargain were simply that the shoplifter had to return the next week and present Pawlak with a church bulletin to verify their attendance. Pawlak's feeling was that a visit to the Lord's house on Sunday was a more effective deterrent than a booking at the Chattanooga Police Department.

It was never entirely clear how successful this strategy was, though certainly not very. Pawlak received a smattering of promised church bulletins. Many of those were surely pilfered from the offender's grandmother or some other family member, so in effect the program may have only succeeded in generating additional thefts. But for the most part, the shoplifters were never seen again, or they were careful to avoid Pawlak on return visits. And yet, he boasted about his rehabilitation strategy as if it were the greatest crime reduction tool ever conceived.

One of Pawlak's shoplifter interventions is expressly seared into my memory. I was in the dreary backroom, shrink-wrapping packages of okra and covering the wilted ones with fresher specimens as I'd been trained, when Pawlak motioned me over to the door. He was peering secretively through the plastic window.

I want you to watch this man, he said.

From that vantage point we could see along the length of the meat aisle. An enormous man was walking—waddling, really—along the railing. He was wearing a capacious pair of tattered overalls and even with his girth, it was clear he had more room in there to stash grocery items. He had a look about him of strained nonchalance—almost as if he were trying a bit too hard to appear unsuspicious.

What about him? I asked.

Pawlak smiled and shook his head. I just watched him take a ham and put it down his overalls, he said.

What? I answered. What are you saying?

He's got a ham, Pawlak repeated. I just saw it. He put it down his overalls into his crotch, and he's going to walk out with it.

A wave of revulsion was sweeping over me as I grasped the scenario. I knew what I would do if I were the manager—which would be absolutely nothing, other than try to somehow scrub the imagery from my mind—but Pawlak was far more dedicated to the cause.

A few minutes later the man weaved his way to the register and paid a few dollars for a some small items in his buggy, the ham still lodged somewhere down between his legs.

As he approached the exit, Pawlak stepped into his path.

Sir, I need a word with you, he said. You didn't pay for your ham.

I don't got no ham, mister.

The man hooked a thumb in the overall straps, defensively. Don't know what you're talking about, he added.

I believe you do, Sir.

Nope.

Pawlak smiled knowingly. These were the moments he lived for, the opportunity to meld Christian compassion with his steely determination to protect Red Food merchandise.

Sir, he said, you and I both know you are hiding a large ham between your legs at this very moment. Now, we can do one of two things. You can be arrested, or you can return the ham to me now.

As he said this, Pawlak slowly reached back and unfastened the handcuffs from his belt loop, jangling them purposefully.

The man flushed a little and lowered his eyes as he realized the jig was up.

I was fixing to pay for it, he said, but I done forgot I had it on me. I'll just give it back to you.

Alright, then, Pawlak said. Now, there's one thing. What we have here is a serious crime. Ordinarily you would be arrested and prosecuted, and you would have a record that will follow you the rest of your life.

Pawlak paused for effect. *The rest of your life*, he said again, with a raised eyebrow and a touch of pity.

But I'm going to give you a choice. If you'll go to church on Sunday—the church of your choice—I won't charge you today. But you agree to come back next week and bring me the church bulletin, so I know you kept your word. Do we have an agreement?

The man could scarcely believe what he was hearing, dumbstruck with elation. He shook his head enthusiastically.

Yes sir, he said. Yes sir, absolutely, that's a deal. I'll go to church, for sure.

They both stood there for a moment uncomfortably.

Oh, yes sir, he said, realizing the moment had come for return of the merchandise.

In one of the more disagreeable scenes I have ever witnessed—before I could think to turn away—he reached down, rooted around in his nether regions for what seemed an eternity, and with a grunt finally retrieved the purloined item. I don't know how much compression it actually takes to deform an eight-pound ham, but he had done it.

Pawlak took possession of the merchandise, clearly delighted with himself. Don't forget—I need that bulletin next week! he shouted encouragingly with a smile as the bandit scurried out the door.

Winking at me as he walked back through the produce department, Pawlak held the ham aloft proudly as if it were the Lombardi trophy.

What are you going to do with that ham? I asked, still battling a touch of nausea.

What do you mean? he asked, and I just waved him on, realizing the question was lost on him.

Of course, the man didn't return. There would be no church bulletin, and I never saw him again. As for the ham, it was back on the meat shelf within minutes. Pawlak knocked a dollar off the price and affixed a bright orange *Manager's Special* sticker to divert attention away from its misshapenness. Just how special it really was, the buyer would never know.

# Chapter 21

## *The Polar Bear Club*

The sole rationale for school, as best I could tell in tenth grade, was to provide a means to play soccer. Thus it only made sense to apply myself at the minimum level necessary to avoid getting suspended from playing sports. At Tennessee Temple if you fell below a C in any class, you were off the team. Probably also Not Right with God. But definitely off the team.

My friend Woody Woodfin and I were poor students who considered C grades to be the pinnacle of success. We were always on the cusp of disqualification. We could study harder, one might argue, but that would require discipline and time.

Manipulating teachers into providing dubious extra credit schemes was the better alternative. It came down to knowing your teacher's limits, which varied greatly from class to class.

On the ruthless end of the spectrum was Mr. Rookberry and his history class. There was no room to maneuver in there. Rookberry was a former Marine who ran his class like a boot camp, only with less frivolity. It was an unnerving environment, especially when he got the crazy eyes, which was six to eight times per hour. We had the sense he was never more than a few seconds from snapping and spraying the class with munitions. Or ejecting students who were Not Right with God through the fifth floor window. Our only choice was to exert a modicum of academic effort in his class in order to maintain the grade.

The other extreme was Mr. Crismond, whose algebra class could best be described as an anarchistic carnival. His philosophy of discipline, it appeared, involved praying in his time off that somehow we would all independently repent, and cease and desist from shooting spitballs at him every time he turned to write an equation on the chalkboard. In his entire career he never sent a single student to detention hall. In Mr. Crismond's moments of greatest exasperation he would threaten to give a pop quiz, but then withdraw the threat in response to vacuous promises of better behavior. As soon as he returned to his board, a staggering array of outrageous mischief would resume instantaneously. Woody and I never passed any examinations in his class and posted some truly appalling test scores which are likely records to this day. And yet, the fix was a snap. We would approach Mr. Crismond mournfully, request extra credit, and promptly be given take-home exercises to rehabilitate our grades. These materials were never completed by either of us personally but instead relayed to classmate coconspirators with more brainpower.

The enigma was Mr. Welborn. On the surface he looked like an easy mark. On the first day of Civics, he mentioned he would not be offering extra credit. I didn't think he was serious about it because he said it with a semblance of a smirk, and with the half-moon eyes and the leisurely gait he never looked like having the energy to enforce anything. Welborn was an oddly amiable fellow who wore a perpetually sleepy countenance. He worked third shift at a publishing company to make ends meet for his family, and though always visibly tired was fond of repeating his axiom that any human could function indefinitely on two hours of sleep per night. Just a matter of willpower, he claimed. I tried it, a few years later in college, but after a few weeks thrashing around numbly on the fringes of consciousness decided it wasn't for me.

Welborn was one of a handful of teachers who seemed to have not quite fully implemented the official Gestapo-esque technique of Christian training. He wanted us to Get Right with God but seemed to sense the process would work better if we got there at our own pace, rather than him trying to make it happen with the cudgel of a rule book and incessant badgering.

Nor was that all that suggested we could have our way with old Welborn. Encouragingly, he was a sports junkie. The man had yet a third gig moonlighting as a radio commentator for local basketball games—you can get a lot done in a twenty-two-hour day—and in class he could be rabbit-trailed away from the lesson at hand to some sports-related debate. The weight of the evidence suggested Welborn's class was one we could safely put on cruise control.

Which was good, because all my energies were focused on the pitch. Woody did the same. We believed we were absolutely indispensable to the success of the Tennessee Temple Crusaders soccer team. Working from his pivotal position at center half, Woody controlled tempo with his physicality, dictating the pace and direction of every attack. From my slot on the right wing, I bedazzled hapless fullbacks with my nimble footwork, delivering silky crosses into the box which were met by our forward Karl, a missionary kid from Brazil with devastating finishing skills heretofore unseen in the hemisphere. That's the way I remember it, at least. Such was our dominance that we hung double digits on several opponents.

It would only be fair, I suppose, to mention that the aforementioned opponents, at this early stage of the season, consisted of ill-conceived, start-up Christian schools whose enrollments were so tiny that every male student they had was required to take the field. While it was rewarding to blow by defenders at will, to be candid they were teams mostly made up of bumbling, bespectacled waifs better suited for the rigors of more tranquil competitions. Like chess or Space Invaders.

But still. There was no denying we were stars, with our own personal fan clubs comprised of almost half a dozen elementary school students who followed us around campus, positively in awe of our greatness.

Soon enough came the opportunity to test Welborn's mettle. Our Civics grades were both knocked down to Ds by an extremely harsh test on Manifest Destiny. I don't recall anymore which one of us copied the other's test, but it was not a bright ploy. And it was an unwelcome distraction because the Baylor game was coming up. Baylor was a prep school stocked with fine, if quite snobby, athletes. They had people to seed their fields and people to bring them Gatorade and people to wash their jocks and people to help with their homework projects and parents who delivered them to school in BMWs. We despised the thought of losing to Baylor.

As it stood, however, with a pair of Ds in Civics we wouldn't be playing.

Fortunately, salvation was at hand in the form of the vaunted *Political News of the Week* Friday oral presentation. It went like this. Every Friday, two students, teamed together, were scheduled to take the entire 50-minute class period to report on the week's political news. The assignment, as Welborn prescribed it, was to read the papers every day, clip news of key events in Washington, summarize them and supply commentary and perspective.

This was a fearful proposition for most, combining leaden

political information with protracted public speaking. Many students were physically ill during the week leading up to their presentations as they spent sleepless nights amassing information and struggling to conjure up a full class period of material. Welborn left it up to each student duo to decide which of them would deliver the oral presentation.

Woody and I were teamed together, and our assigned presentation was happily slated for the Friday before the Tuesday Baylor game. A solid performance would lift us back up to Cs, where we belonged.

I was good at research but not keen on the public speaking. Woody, meanwhile, was a popular conversationalist in any crowd, albeit not exactly renowned for staying on topic.

I'll do the research, you do the presentation, I said.

OK, Woody said, but I feel better presenting my own material. I'll take care of everything.

OK, I said.

It wouldn't be correct to say I thought a lot more about this in the days leading up to the presentation, but I did ask Woody a couple of times how the preparation was going, and the responses were vague and disconcerting.

I'm not worried about it, he said.

What are you doing to get ready? I asked.

What do you mean? he replied. It's just Welborn.

I suppose, I countered, but you have to talk about something.

I will, he said.

On Thursday Coach Bindler asked us if our grades were in order.

Everything will be fine, said Woody, after our Civics presentation tomorrow.

We're in good shape, I added.

AT THE APPOINTED HOUR, Woody ambled to the front with his Trapper Keeper and opened it on the teacher's stand. He retrieved a fistful of dog-eared newspaper articles and proceeded to read them verbatim, following each piece with extensive, off-the-cuff commentary. He was witty and expansive and funny and the class was fully engaged. The only thing was that neither his articles nor his commentary had even the remotest connection to the subject of civics.

His first submission was a *USA Today* account of a dog who had been lost by his family on the east coast while on vacation. Three years later, the animal arrived back home in Washington State, mange-infested and hungry but otherwise OK. Woody wandered out of this story into a detailed reminisce about his own bird dog and a recent squirrel hunting expedition. He recounted several incidents of escalating fascination and the tale seemed to be building to a crescendo, but ended disappointingly when Woody reported that *we didn't get no squirrel and went back home.*

This generated much amusement, and I watched Welborn for signs of an impending intervention, but he sat mutely in the back of the room, grading papers, the ever-present half smile on his lips.

Woody's next submission was from the local paper, a report of an unfortunate gentleman who had been transported to the hospital after accidentally slicing open his own neck with a chainsaw while cutting firewood. The way Woody reported it made the gruesome accident somehow comical, and this was followed by his personal views on dumb city people who shouldn't be running power tools and then, inexplicably, he somehow segued to an account of his recent work in helping his grandfather remove a pig's testicles. The procedure wasn't performed with a chainsaw and it was difficult to see how this had anything to do with anything, but this was the way Woody's mind worked and it was wondrous to behold. Especially as an alternative to discussing whatever bill Tip O'Neil might have pushed through Congress in the last week.

Woody covered several more arcane stories, then reported the prior week's NFL scores and read a segment from *Leonard's Losers*, a local newsletter offering betting tips on the upcoming week's games. And then came the *piece de resistance*.

It was an extensive feature article on the Polar Bear Club, an association of geezers in New York who assembled for the express purpose of subjecting themselves to swims in the frigid waters off Coney Island. Holding up the paper for all to see, there didn't seem to be much substance to the report. A couple of paragraphs and two halftones of octogenarian nutjubs splashing around. But Woody had ten minutes left to fill in his presentation, and fill it he did, with an amazingly brilliant, incoherent and circuitous ramble. He gave his opinion of the limited mental abilities of Northerners in general and the Polar Bear clubbers in particular. He wandered off to a tale about the time the ice froze on a pond over in Dade County and how one of the fat kids had fallen through. He speculated on the severity of the coming winter and how the *Farmer's Almanac* was infinitely more dependable than the local weatherman on Channel 9, who was wrong about the forecast most every day and, in Woody's assessment, wouldn't have the sense to pound sand down a rathole. This reminded him that the station's sports anchor, Darrell Patterson, had recently gotten a perm. Woody noted that it was—in his humble but unassailable opinion—distinctly lacking in manliness. He allowed, however, that he liked Darrell nevertheless because Darrell did a good job of covering Major League Baseball. From there he jumped inevitably to his hero, Pete Rose, who would never get a perm and, in any event, his hair appeared to be made of straw and would be unlikely to succumb to any attempts to reshape it, even if he tried. Which again, he wouldn't. You'll never see Pete Rose in hair curlers, I promise you that, he said. There was then a foray, naturally, into the art of base stealing and only after that conversation had been thoroughly vetted—and now, remembering his original topic—Woody spoke at length about how difficult it would be to play baseball in the winter because you can't keep your muscles warmed up and you would be pulling muscles with every throw or even, God forbid, pull a hamstring stealing third. Like I did last year, he said. There's nothing worse than pulling a hammy.

There was a moment of silence as he thought about how he could possibly close this out. He reached back into his pile of dog-eared clippings and held up the Polar Bear Club article again, and we took a final look at the photos of the old men frolicking in the ocean.

I don't know if they pulled any hamstrings, but them boys are crazy, Woody said.

And with that, he returned to his seat, to robust and sustained applause. Despite having covered an astounding wealth of material, he had managed to get through his civics presentation without once coming within a country mile of any political topic. He had been everywhere with his remarks, it seemed, except Washington, D.C.

Mr. Welborn sauntered to the front of the classroom. As always, he appeared to be mildly amused.

Thank you Woody, he said. It was entertaining, I'll grant you that.

---

It was Monday, the day before the Baylor game, when Woody and I were cornered in the hallway by a bristling Coach Bindler. There was a note in my box, he said through clenched teeth, that you two both still have a D in Civics.

What? I said. That can't be right.

We'll take care of it, said Woody.

You better, Coach replied.

We arrived a few minutes early for Civics. Welborn was sitting at his desk. It would be a simple matter. Feign humility, apologize, offer to do some extra work. Welborn would chastise us, assign a makeup task, and then bump us up to C's.

Gentlemen? he said as we approached.

We need your help, Woody said meekly. You know the Baylor game is tomorrow?

Right, he said. Who are they going to put in your spots?

I laughed nervously at the little joke.

Mr. Welborn, I said, we were hoping you could give us some extra credit. We've been struggling a bit in Civics but we're willing to try harder. But this game tomorrow is really important.

Can't do it, he said. The slight smile was on his lips again, and this time I noticed it seem to have a sinister element to it.

You have to, Woody said. You have to, please.

Gentleman, Welborn said, I told you on day one I don't offer extra credit.

But this is Baylor, I said.

And this is Civics, he answered coldly.

You can't be serious, Woody countered. Without us, we'll lose for sure.

I know, Welborn said, and it's unfortunate, because it certainly will be your fault. The blame is going to fall on the two of you, there's no question.

What about our presentation? Woody asked. Can't we get extra credit for the presentation?

Welborn looked skyward, mystically.

No, Mr. Woodfin, I cannot offer any extra credit for your presentation, enlightening though it was.

What was wrong with it? Woody asked innocently.

The Polar Bear Club? Welborn said with a touch of disdain. With all due respect, Mr. Woodfin, I wasn't able to ascertain the linkage between the Polar Bear Club and any impending legislation. Same with the squirrels, and Pete Rose, et cetera. Accordingly, you and Mr. Ray have each been given an F for the presentation.

It went on for a few more minutes. We appealed with every argument we could muster, from school spirit to the doctrine of grace to shameless declarations about how he was our favorite teacher and that we had really, really been trying hard to Get Right with God. They all hit a brick wall. As every argument bounced off, the reality became inescapable: Welborn had been misjudged.

Woody and I watched from the sidelines as Baylor thumped us, 3-0. Who knows if we would have made any difference, but we had served ourselves up as the objects of culpability. At the team meeting following the match Coach Bindler went into a frenzy about how our irresponsibility was the proximate cause of the loss. How we had let our teammates down.

In another couple of weeks we had pulled our grades up to Cs and were permitted to rejoin the team. Bindler commemorated our return by making everybody run endless line drills until several people disgorged their lunch.

When two people screw up, everybody suffers, he said. We are a team.

I hated Welborn for a good long while. We had a few more

classes with him in the ensuing years and somewhere deep inside we began to understand that all the while, he was teaching us something more than Civics.

For years afterward I thought about him now and then, the feelings softening as the years rolled on. And then I found out he was dying of cancer. I sent a few notes, trying to reassure him his life's work wasn't totally wasted. Neither Woody nor I were incarcerated and were trying to make something good out of our lives. His replies were full of heart and there was a gentleness and gentlemanliness and generosity about him.

You know something? Woody said to me after the news came that Old Welborn had gone to heaven. He was probably one of the only teachers at that school who really loved us.

# Chapter 22

## *The Pickle Contest*

I WAS SCHEDULED TO BE OFF WORK SATURDAY BUT HERE was Pedro calling, saying I needed to be at Red Food promptly at six a.m. for an emergency meeting called by Mr. Crumpler.

What emergency? I asked.

I don't know, Pedro replied, but it sounds serious.

Who has to be there?

Everybody, he said. Everybody who works at Red Food #100 has to be here.

By now I was accustomed to these ad hoc meetings, which were typically announced with a degree of solemnity suggesting something monumental would occur. The subject matter was never revealed beforehand, but you were warned your career in the Red Food empire depended on your attendance. This was a standard Red Food management tack—summoning employees to inconveniently-scheduled, mandatory meetings for which we were not allowed to clock in—designed to reinforce in our minds that we were powerless serfs who toiled at the pleasure and whim of management.

And once you arrived at the meeting—having given up

sleep, a class, a date, soccer practice, whatever—you discovered the meeting had nothing to do with you. Maybe there would be an announcement that so and so had been fired. Such news would have been disseminated soon enough without any meeting, but the fear could be ratcheted up by formalizing the message. You'll be next if you don't step it up, was the takeaway.

Part-timers like me considered these meetings to be banal and irrelevant, not to mention extremely annoying. But Red Food career people like Pedro were terrified every time one was scheduled, because being jettisoned by Red Food spelled the end of your grocery career. The company's complete domination of the tri-state market meant there was nowhere else to turn. Screw this up, and you're throwing newspapers in the wee hours.

Pedro's lip was quivering noticeably when I arrived. We joined a group of concerned employees in the backroom who were milling around nervously, puzzling over what they could have done wrong this time. Presently Mr. Crumpler strode into the room, face aglow with his usual contrived joviality.

GREAT TO SEE YOU ALL HERE, he bellowed. THE REASON WE'RE HAVING THIS HERE MEETING TODAY IS TO LET YOU KNOW THAT THE WHOLE RED FOOD CHAIN IS HAVING A PICKLE CONTEST, TO SEE WHICH STORE CAN SELL THE MOST PICKLES. AND STORE #100 IS AIMING TO WIN IT!

The emergency is to announce a pickle contest? Rage boiled up in me but before I could further ponder the absurdity, my thoughts were drowned out as Crumpler continued his soliloquy.

EVERY ONE OF US HAS TO WORK TOGETHER. WE'RE GOING TO MOVE MORE PICKLES THAN WE EVER HAVE BEFORE. I KNOW RED FOOD STORE

#100 CAN DO IT! I NEED EVERY DEPARTMENT TO SET UP PICKLE DISPLAYS.

WE'RE GOING TO MOVE PICKLES IN PRODUCE.

WE'RE GOING TO MOVE PICKLES IN DAIRY.

WE'RE GOING TO MOVE PICKLES IN THE MEAT DEPARTMENT.

Mr. Crumpler paused for a moment and glanced at the faces around the room to gauge the level of excitement. There was none. So he turned up the volume and carried on.

THIS IS ABOUT MORE THAN PICKLES. THIS IS ABOUT RED FOOD PRIDE. WHEN THIS CONTEST ENDS, EVERY ONE OF YOU IS GONNA BE PROUD TO KNOW YOU'RE PART OF THE BEST STORE IN THIS WHOLE COMPANY. RED FOOD #100 IS GOING TO SHOW ALL THE OTHER RED FOODS HOW TO SELL PICKLES.

He blasted out some further nonsense about how he had painstakingly assembled the best staff in the history of Red Food right here at this store, conveniently ignoring the well-known fact that most of the employees had been exiled here by corporate. He hadn't assembled anything. Finally, he ended with a question which turned out to be hypothetical since it was instantaneously followed by his signature exclamation.

EVERYBODY ON BOARD? GREAT!

And then he wheeled around and vanished behind the swing door.

I turned to Pedro, who was flush with relief that the subject matter hadn't involved a personal reprimand or termination.

But I had questions. Why was Mr. Crumpler obsessed with a pickle contest we surely could not win? Ours was the second-smallest store in the chain and had zero chance of outselling the others in pickles or any other product. And how exactly would we sell pickles in the produce department?

Maybe we can tie-in to cucumbers, said Pedro, with a jagged chuckle. You know? Showing the before and after?

I sighed and went home to salvage what was left of my day off.

The next day I arrived for work to find a veritable pickle kingdom under construction. Mr. Crumpler was hanging a stupendous *Enjoy Mt. Olive Pickles* banner which spanned four aisles near the entrance. Under that was a towering display, constructed of forty or fifty cases of the product. Customers were compelled to negotiate an awkward ninety degree turn around the stuff just to get their buggies down the aisle.

In produce, Pedro was dutifully hanging a sign on his own display, stacked high in front of the produce scales, so that every shopper bringing fruits or vegetables to be weighed would be confronted by the pickles.

Sawyer the butcher seethed with bitterness on the best of days, and the pickle decree had done nothing to brighten his mood. He was muscling some Mt. Olive boxes in the vicinity of the hot dogs, which at least seemed to have some marginal correlation. With a touch of sarcasm, I asked him if he was excited about the pickle contest. He responded with a stream of profanity concerning Mr. Crumpler which culminated with a recommendation of monogenesis.

Over by the milk coolers the Mayfield Dairy Farms vendor was about to come to blows with Toby the stock boy, who had reduced visibility of Mayfield products to zero with a wall of pickle boxes.

What are these pickles doing here? demanded the Mayfield man.

Mr. Crumpler wants 'em here, Toby replied.

But this ain't got nothing to do with dairy! How am I supposed to sell any product when the customers can't see it?

Mr. Crumpler says pickles and ice cream go together, Toby replied authoritatively.

The Mayfield man stormed off to take his battle to Crumpler. But when it was over, the pickles stayed.

Everywhere, everywhere, were the pickles. In a store that sold maybe a couple of cases of pickles a week, Crumpler had ordered endless pallets of the stuff.

Soon after beginning my shift, Mr. Crumpler ambled through produce. PICKLE DISPLAY IS GREAT, he said. BE SURE YOU ASK EVERY CUSTOMER IF THEY NEED PICKLES.

Say, Mr. Crumpler, I asked, hoping to get some insight into his obsession with the contest. Why is this pickle thing so important?

He chafed at the question, face reddening like Super Mario under attack from a flame chomp. BECAUSE WE WANT TO BE THE BEST, IS WHY. THAT'S WHAT STORE #100 IS ALL ABOUT, BEING THE BEST.

The whole thing was baffling, but Crumpler kept the pressure on everyone, delivering furious admonishments to any employee who failed to suggest a pickle purchase with every customer interaction.

For their part, the shoppers began having visceral reactions to the contest. Every visit to the store involved at least five or six solicitations, navigating aisles transformed into perplexing pickle display mazes, and irritating public address announcements every five minutes broadcast by Mr. Crumpler, whose thunderous voice reached weapons-grade when boosted by a speaker system.

One elderly gent, standing at the produce scales as I weighed his bananas, summed up the general sentiment when he looked skyward as another of Crumpler's sales pitches came booming down from the PA.

What's got into that fellar? he asked. A person can't eat but so many pickles.

A few days later we got the answer from a visiting district supervisor, who let it slip that the manager of the store selling the most pickles would win a trip to Hawaii.

Does our store have a chance of winning? I asked.

Not in a million years, he laughed.

For three weeks, the contest continued. I, for one, sold very few jars of pickles. And yet, the most remarkable thing happened.

By the grace of God, I was already at work when another of Crumpler's emergency meetings was called.

Crumpler was positively over the moon. RED FOOD #100 DID IT! WE WON THE PICKLE CONTEST!

By this time, most of the employees knew the whole thing was really about seven days and six nights in Oahu for Crumpler and his wife—but he didn't know we knew.

Sawyer the butcher, pulling on a Marlboro in the back of the room, made an effort to draw out a confession.

What do we win? he asked.

Crumpler stuttered for a moment, then mustered up a spirited response.

I'LL TELL YOU WHAT WE WON, he answered. WE WON THE KNOWLEDGE THAT WE'RE BETTER THAN THE REST. I ALREADY KNEW YOU WERE THE BEST, BUT NOW EVERYBODY KNOWS IT!

Sawyer took one more stab at it.

Yeah, but is there a prize?

THIS CONTEST WAS NEVER ABOUT PRIZES. IT WAS ABOUT RED FOOD PRIDE, AND WE DONE PROVED WE GOT THE MOST. AND I'M PROUD OF EVERY ONE OF YOU. EVERY ONE OF YOU IS GREAT!

For several weeks, the unexpected victory was the subject

of intense speculation. None of the employees with whom I conferred remembered selling more than a few jars of pickles. The mountainous displays hadn't seemed to dwindle much during the contest and the cashiers didn't report many Mt. Olive jars coming down the conveyer belt.

And yet, somehow Crumpler was on his way to Hawaii.

---

I FOUND THEM BY ACCIDENT, late one night, when a colleague threw my price gun on top of a giant backroom cooler as a prank. I fetched a ladder to retrieve it, and once on top discovered I had a panoramic view of the vast storeroom. In a shadowy corner, hidden from sight at ground level by some strategically discarded grocery shelving, were case upon case upon case of Mt. Olive pickles.

In the day before computerized inventories and bar codes tracked sales, Mr. Crumpler had simply secreted away most of the pickles ordered from the warehouse and reported them as sold.

After he returned from Hawaii all tanned and jolly, Sawyer the butcher orchestrated a quiet campaign to undermine Crumpler by badmouthing him to various district managers. He complained—not exactly cryptically—that he needed more storage space, but the pallets of Mt. Olive pickles left over from the competition were in the way. During future contests, district managers took to surveying the backroom on their visits to keep Crumpler honest.

The following autumn Red Food launched another competition, this one for Diamond Walnuts. Having been told I was an amateur artist, Crumpler ordered me to paint a giant squirrel on a thirty-foot wide banner to stimulate customer interest in walnuts. But my skills had been overstated. I didn't get the tail quite right, and the squirrel looked more like a rat, which brought a wave of derision. It may have also acted to suppress sales for the entire store, let alone the walnuts, as the overhanging image of an immense rodent is probably not the way to set the stage for incoming shoppers.

After he lost, Crumpler placed the blame on me, chewing me out, ironically, in the very backroom where the expired pickles were still stacked in the corner collecting dust.

YOUR SQUIRREL COST US FROM WINNING THE NUT COMPETITION, he bellowed. IS THAT THE BEST SQUIRREL YOU COULD HAVE PAINTED?

Probably not, Sir, I said.

THEN THAT THERE'S THE PROBLEM. IF YOU WANT TO BE NUMBER ONE, he said, YOU GOTTA BE WILLING TO GO THE EXTRA MILE.

Looking over his shoulder toward the countless boxes of Mt. Olive pickles reaching high to the ceiling, it was clear to me how deeply he meant it.

# Chapter 23

## *Jesus and the Timberlands*

I COULD NEVER FIND A DECENT PAIR OF SHOES GROWING up. My feet were always out of proportion to the rest of my body and were embarrassingly wide and difficult to fit. In England the shoe salesmen accustomed to serving pocket-sized Scotsmen would marvel at the dimensions registering on the foot measuring device, and then look up to my mom and say with great exasperation: We don't have that size, Missus.

On the few visits when they did have the right size, it was usually a hideous pair that had been unsellable through several generations, like something Clement Attlee would have worn, and not anything suitable for Kingswood School. The only acceptable fashion there was the style popularized by Sid Vicious and Johnny Rotten—big, black monstrosities with thick, heavy soles which doubled as effective weapons in a fight.

I had made the mistake of showing up for school one day in a set of Hush Puppies brought over from America. Going in I entertained the idea my classmates might be awed by the innovative fashion statement and envisioned myself as a trendsetter, but instead the shoes were immediately classified as loser paraphernalia and I spent the day scrambling to avoid having my face kicked in.

Thankfully my parents eventually recognized my unwieldy feet as a mainspring of great shame and potential suffering, and they decided to break the budget when it came to my shoes. This is how, later in high school, I came into possession of a magnificent pair of Timberlands.

Under normal circumstances I would have no prayer of owning Timberlands. They were far too costly and couldn't be purchased at the likes of Woolworths or Kmart where we normally shopped. But my expansive feet always quickly broke through the cheap materials of discount shoes, and it was decided that investing in shoes of genuine quality would be more economical in the long run.

You better take care of these shoes, said Mom, because we can't afford to be buying Timberlands on a whim.

The warning was unnecessary because I loved those shoes. They were warm and comfortable and stylish and no one made fun of you in Timberlands.

———

I WAS WEARING them on the night we went to the Pacific Garden Mission. For reasons I no longer remember, our class voted to go to Chicago for our senior trip even though it was March and freezing cold. The sun never gave a hint of making an appearance the whole time we were there, but we had a grand old time anyway. That is, right up until the moment the teachers decided we should go down to Whiskey Row on State Street to have a look at what would happen to us if we didn't listen to them about the perils of consuming alcohol and listening to rock music.

Other classes went to Jamaica or at least Fort Lauderdale

and came back with dazzling tans and stirring tales of decadence. Our class visited the homeless.

We all exited the bus and passed under a mammoth, bright yellow neon cross. It loomed above the entryway of the old building with the words *Jesus Saves* lighting up the sky. We filed into the miserable auditorium for the evening service. The place was ancient and reeked of a foul blend of pasta and body odor, with homeless men ambling about in various states of consciousness. Eventually the mission staff settled them down into their seats for the mandatory pre-dinner gospel meeting.

There was a hymn or two, with about nobody singing or paying attention, and then the preacher went after it for thirty minutes or so. I was in my usual state of detachment and transported myself mentally to a faraway soccer field. In due course the sermon came to an end and the invitation began.

A trickle of men staggered forward and were motioned into the counseling room. Maybe there was the hope of a double portion of noodles or something for making a decision, I don't know. But then the preacher did something unexpected—something that created something of a panic among the senior boys of Tennessee Temple Academy.

I'd like to ask a few of the young men visiting with us tonight to come on up and share the gospel with those who have come forward, he said.

Mr. Welborn stood hesitantly and scanned the room. I cannot imagine the hopelessness that must have swept over him at the prospect of having to select three or four of his senior students who would be capable of meeting this challenge. As a group we were exceptionally unqualified to share anything with anyone, let alone present the gospel to inebriated men triple our age.

There was one exception. Wayne Powell, who had already committed his life to the ministry, sprang into action immediately. But Mr. Welborn needed a few more counselors. Along with everyone else I slid low in my chair, trying to make myself very small.

It was no good. I heard my name called. With a painful dearth of choices, I had been deemed a workable evangelist. Welborn assumed I at least could rattle off some verses and get through it.

Begrudgingly and fearfully I arose and proceeded to the counseling room. This is a good way to get stabbed to death on your senior trip, I thought to myself. The preacher pointed me toward a seat next to an old African-American man who looked like utter hell. It was time to close the sale, so to speak.

I offered a hand and introduced myself. His hand was tremorous and cold and felt like sandpaper. The eyes were yellow and he smelled bad and what few teeth he had left were rotting. An old red ball cap perched on his head was so soiled and tattered I contemplated briefly if it had passed through the digestive system of some large animal before he had acquired it.

I asked him where he was from.

Right here in Chicago, he answered.

Yeah, this is a nice town, I stuttered, before realizing how dumb a thing that was to say to a homeless man.

I perceived we were not going to have a lot of common ground to discuss, so I moved right in with the Ask.

Would you like to be saved? I said tentatively.

Sure would, he said. But I was wundrin' about something.

Now I was worried. If we were going to get into any type of deep theological discussion, I was going to be found wanting. If he was wundrin' about the intricacies of Calvinism or the spirit gifts or the doctrine of sanctification, I was going to have little of substance for him and promptly be exposed as an incompetent.

But he wasn't wundrin' about any of that. His raised a gnarled hand to his face and massaged the stubble on his chin.

What kind of shoes is those you have on there?

I looked down at my feet. It seemed like an out-of-place question, what with his eternal security hanging in the balance at this very instant.

Well, I replied, these are called Timberland shoes.

Uh-huh, he said. I like those.

Me too, I said. Timberland makes nice shoes. Now, let me show you a verse, sir.

I opened my Bible to John 3:16.

You see here, sir, this verse talks about how Jesus loved the whole world—you and me included—and died for us so that we could have a home in heaven. It says right here that if you believe in Him, you can have everlasting life. Do you believe that?

He was still looking down at the floor.

Well, I don't know, he said. A sigh, and another rub of the whiskers. Say again what it is that you call them shoes? Timberman?

No, it's Timberlands, sir. Timberlands.

Timberlands, he repeated. Timberlands. I like those shoes. Yes sir, I sure do. That's a nice pair of shoes.

I bit my lip a little in frustration. I was trying to rescue the man from the clutches of hell and he was fixated on shoes. The old change of subject gambit. And yet I knew I didn't want to go back to Welborn to report failure and thus be responsible for chalking one up in the ledger for Satan.

I put my hand on his shoulder and tried to draw him back in.

Now let me ask you something, I said. Would you like to have that gift of everlasting life? All you have to do is ask. Jesus says it right here in the book of John, that if you believe in Him, you will have everlasting life. A new life, really. All you have to do is pray and ask Jesus to forgive you of your sins and save you.

Yeah, I could do that I guess, he answered absently. He was still looking down at the floor.

This is not getting through, I thought to myself, even while growing in determination to get him through this sinner's prayer if it would be the last thing I did. But just as I opened my mouth, he was at it again with another inquiry about the Timberlands.

How much do a pair of shoes like that run? he asked, his voice suffused with a touch of innocence.

Now I was starting to get aggravated.

Um, I don't know, I said. My mom bought them for me actually. I think they were like forty dollars or something like that.

He reared back a little, shocked that any pair of shoes could run that high. I felt awkward, and the sudden need to defend the exorbitance.

But they're good shoes, I said. I hardly ever buy shoes, and these will last a long time. Years, even.

He nodded. Yes, sir, I can see that. A pair of shoes like that would last a good long time, yes sir.

He looked into my eyes briefly and then lowered his head again.

Back to salvation I went again.

If you want to accept Christ, you can just say these words, repeat after me, I said. Not waiting for another diversion to the Timberlands, I quickly led him in the sinner's prayer, and he mumbled perfunctorily through it.

We sat there together for a minute, neither saying anything. Around us there were other people praying, mumbling. The pasta smell was stronger here. Must be closer to the kitchen, I thought.

Anyway, mission accomplished, finally. I was ready to get

going, report my success, breathe in something other than this rank, oppressive air.

He pursed his lips and rubbed the back of his neck. Still he was looking down at my feet. For a man who had just accepted the gift of eternal life, he didn't seem to be noticeably different.

I bet a pair of shoes like those is warm, isn't they?

Anybody else would have figured it out earlier, but it was only then I realized what he wanted.

I looked down at his boots, what was left of them. Mud-encrusted relics, cracked and warped. One of them didn't have a shoelace, and there was a big tear on the side and his sock was poking through like a hernia.

They were big, wide shoes. Looked to be about my size.

I had a number of thoughts, in that moment when I realized the old man wanted my Timberlands, and I've always been sorry none of them really had much to do with him.

The first one involved the specter of me walking out of the Pacific Garden Mission, onto the sidewalk, and onto the bus, in my socks. I would be a laughingstock. At some points in your life you don't mind being a laughingstock. But when you're in high school, you mind.

Not to mention it was cold—really cold. I had a pair of Stan Smiths back at the hotel, but they were not really suitable for wearing all the time. Not cool. And what was I going to say to Mom? Oh, yeah, by the way, those Timberlands you bought— the ones that have to last for a couple years—I gave them to some hobo in Chicago.

And one more thing, I thought. This was after all the Pacific Garden Mission. This gent was about to get a hot meal, a warm bed if he wanted it, and no doubt they had a whole room full of shoes stacked up back in there somewhere for people like him. More than likely he was working me over for these Timberlands and would convert them to cash and liquor before the heater warmed up the bus.

And still, there was that hole in his shoe, with the sock sticking out, and the numbing cold outside.

I didn't know what to do, and then while I was trying to decide, suddenly it was time to go. The service was over, our bus was leaving, the men were lining up for dinner. I almost slipped off my Timberlands, but I didn't.

I stood up. God bless you sir, I said. He just looked at me.

I walked away.

Probably, he just responded to the altar call so he could take a crack at conning some naïve kid out of a pair of expensive shoes. It hadn't worked out for him this time.

Or maybe. Maybe he listened to me tell him how Jesus could change his life, and then I left him there with busted boots with a big hole in the side and a missing shoelace.

That's what I was afraid of.

---

ON THE RIDE back to the hotel, everybody was talking about how glad they were to be done with the trip to the Pacific Garden Mission. I can't believe Welborn picked you to be one of the counselors, they were saying. You, of all people. Never would have called that one.

After the guffaws died down a little, I pressed my face against the bus window and blurred my eyes so the lights, and the buildings, and the people would be all muddled as they flickered by in the darkness.

All I could think of was that I should have given him my Timberlands.

## Chapter 24

## *The Great Buggy Repossession*

Jack Nicholson was creepy in *The Shining* and some people were having nightmares about the Overlook Hotel, but for me the Jaycee Towers and its occupants served up more horror than anything conjured by Hollywood.

Red Food Store #100 provided wretched working conditions on any day of the week, but Thursdays were the worst. That was the day local churches in downtown Chattanooga, in a great ecumenical charitable collaboration, drove their buses and vans to the Jaycee Towers to pick up the elderly and shuttle them to our store. Just up the hill and looming ominously over Red Food, the Towers were part of a government-subsidized retirement complex housing hundreds of senior citizens.

When you are a produce clerk whose job it is to stock and maintain the fruits and vegetables in an orderly and appealing array, there is nothing quite so terrifying as the elderly. They inspect every piece of fruit, poking and prodding with fanatical zeal. They monopolize your time. They ask questions that would stump a biochemist, and they hold you personally responsible for the quality of the merchandise. It was not uncommon to find yourself expending fifteen minutes defending the origin of an orange against the allegations of a single cane-wielding customer.

Every grocery store employee wrangles with the odd cantankerous customer, but Thursday mornings at Red Food were something from another realm entirely because the retirees were released upon us in packs. Thanks to the churches and their free transportation, the entire population of the Jaycee Towers was dumped into the store at once.

Pedro didn't tell me what was coming, that first time. I was thinking it had the makings of a slow morning, ignorant of what was about to happen. We were standing there enjoying a sedate conversation at the produce scales counter when—glancing out the front window—he abruptly stiffened and mumbled something about needing to get some paperwork done in the back room. A moment after he fled, a wave of slow-moving but purposeful seniors surged into the produce department.

In an instant I was surrounded and demands came flying in from all sides. One infuriated customer waved a leaking paper bag in my face, charging me with selling rotten peaches. Several others simultaneously ordered me to fetch the fresher product from the back, adamant we were secreting away the top-quality stuff. One gent pointedly mentioned his close personal friendship with the store manager before demanding I plug a watermelon, which he needed immediately. Before I could respond to him, a cadaverous old woman standing at the dry bin held an onion aloft in her fist and began yelling at me over the other plaintive voices. She was physically shaking with anger, fixing me with an eye that could not have been eviler if I had personally terminated the entire social security program.

Sonny, she sneered, this is no more a Vidalia onion than I am!

Just then another customer lost control of his buggy, struck the banana stand a glancing blow, and careered into a flimsy display holding boxes of vanilla wafers. It promptly toppled, depositing the whole lot of them on the floor in a wide arc.

All of this happened in the opening moments, and still they were streaming in. And as I looked with despair beyond the front door, additional buses were pulling up and yet more of them were eagerly disembarking.

I was quickly going into shock but was brought back around by a smart tug of my sleeve and a shrill voice projecting directly into my left ear canal.

Hey! Hey! Hey! Mister!

I turned to see a frail-looking woman at my elbow. She wasn't quite five feet tall but wore a menacing expression suggesting she would level me if I did not attend to her first. I deduced she was almost deaf—judging by the stentorian voice with which she was addressing me from point blank range—and her question would reveal an additional infirmity:

Mister, where are the glycerin suppositories?

Naively, I left my station to aid her in finding this product, and she bullied me into retrieving numerous other items as well. By the time I got back to the produce department, the scale of devastation was tornadic. Bruised and torn fruits and vegetables were flung every which way. The shattered remains of a cantaloupe lay ruptured hazardously on the floor. Before I could make any further assessment, the angry swarm convened upon me again.

---

An hour or so later when it was finally over, I was physically and emotionally wrecked and contemplating resignation. Virtually every customer had been outraged, and it wasn't just that they believed I was inept. They alleged I was also a produce charlatan, a merchant of fraud whose decided mission was to deceive them into buying inferior grade fruits and vegetables at inflated prices. One gent alleged I was trying to kill him so he would be unable to report my fleecing operation.

Mr. Crumpler would be hearing the complaints—they made that much clear. I didn't see how things would be GREAT when they were done with him.

Pedro appeared from the back room with a warped grin. So, uh, did you have fun with the Towers people? he asked with a touch of cruelty.

Well, I'm going to be fired, I said. As soon as they get over to Mr. Crumpler and report what they think of me, I'm a goner.

No, no, no, he replied. This is normal ... happens every week. This is the way they shop. Besides, Pedro continued, Mr. Crumpler has got a lot more problems with the Towers people than anything happening in produce.

And Pedro was right about that, because a protracted dispute between Mr. Crumpler and the people from the Towers was about to boil over.

---

Some of the elderly residents were in better shape than others. The spry ones had the option of shopping at Red Food more than just the one time each week when free transportation was offered. They could walk down the hill to the store any time they fancied. But even the hale and hearty among them struggled to negotiate the return trip, back up the hill, with arms full of groceries. The obvious solution was to wheel their purchases all the way home in a Red Food shopping buggy. The issue for Mr. Crumpler was that the buggies were seldom returned.

With every passing day the supply of buggies at the store dwindled, and it soon it became a crisis. Shoppers would enter the store during busy periods to find there was nothing to put their groceries in. The Towers people were threatening to decimate Mr. Crumpler's already-paltry store sales.

It was time to take action, and Mr. Crumpler summoned his loyal sidekick, Boyd.

A pleasant kid who had distinguished himself in his service to Red Food through hard work and sycophancy, Boyd had worked himself up to the position of head bag boy. The formula for reaching this pinnacle of success involved saying *Yes Sir* instantly to any request, being on time, continuing to work for an hour or two after clocking out, volunteering for unpleasant jobs, and generally attending to the whims of the store manager. Above all the head bag boy had to be trustworthy and loyal—he might know where all the pickles were buried, but he would never tell.

A feature of this position involved being plied, on a regular basis, with the promise that you were on the fast track to a Red Food management position. This was, naturally, a complete lie. There was an oft-cited anecdote about one employee who purportedly rose from the rank of bag boy to store manager, but after inquiring as to the details I learned the individual's journey up the corporate ladder took about twenty years, and he had some helpful shoves from his brother who was a district manager for the bakery department.

The other benefit of the head bag boy position—the real one—was that you no longer had to bag groceries, except in crises, or to train a rookie.

When Boyd heard his name over the intercom, he dutifully sprinted to the front of the store.

Yes Sir, Mr. Crumpler! Boyd reported enthusiastically, the sweat pouring off his face. Boyd was a profoundly rotund youngster—almost completely round, really—and his constant dashing about generated a torrential volume of perspiration. He was soaked through round the clock—even his red bow tie was soggy.

Mr. Crumpler placed a hand on his protégé's shoulder. BOYD, THEM OLD PEOPLE UP AT THE TOWERS HAVE GOT ALL OUR BUGGIES. RUN UP THERE AND SEE IF YOU CAN FIND SOME AND BRING 'EM BACK.

A ripple of chagrin stole across Boyd's face. He had plenty of experience facing the wrath of senior shoppers, and you could see his mind trying to analyze the range of invidious reprisals he might be subjected to upon confronting them on their own turf. But quickly he snapped himself back into loyal minion mode. Yes Sir, Mr. Crumpler! he said, all but saluting, and away he went up the hill.

There was an uncomfortable wait for his return. I thought the most likely outcome would be that Boyd would be dismembered and his remains flushed down a toilet somewhere up there, but at length he reappeared at the crest of the hill, piloting a train of buggies. He wheeled them through the front door and collapsed in a heap by the express lane. Several minutes passed before he caught his breath enough to give an account of his mission.

The scene up at the Towers, Boyd reported, was an alarming one. He had corralled what buggies he could, but others were being put to bizarre uses or otherwise irretrievable. Some were being employed as mobile plant holders, rolling laundry hampers, and portable dumpsters. Most disturbingly, one resident had divulged that a cache of buggies was locked in a storage room, and Boyd was told flatly Red Food wasn't getting them back under any circumstances.

Mr. Crumpler took all this in, gradually realizing he had a

tricky problem on his hands. The people at the Towers believed their occasional shopping trips to Red Food entitled them to ownership of the buggies. He could send Boyd up on regular recovery missions, but as they were put to other uses or hidden away up at the old folks' enclave, his supply of buggies would inevitably continue to decline.

The solution came for Mr. Crumpler in a conversation with his supervisor at the corporate office. In some musty warehouse, it was revealed, Red Food had a stash of old buggies—hundreds of them. They had been retired from service and were no longer needed. Here was the perfect remedy to all his problems: Red Food would donate some of these old buggies to the senior citizens. The store's buggies would be retrieved, the Towers residents would be delighted to have their own special buggies and—best of all—Mr. Crumpler and Red Food would surely be credited for their magnanimous gesture in support of the elderly.

THIS IS GREAT! Mr. Crumpler announced exuberantly, in another of his hastily called emergency meetings. THE OLD PEOPLE WIN. RED FOOD WINS. EVERYBODY WILL BE HAPPY.

He didn't say it, but you could see Mr. Crumpler was thinking this just might be the thing to push his career into the stratosphere. He likely envisioned the Towers residents showering him with praise on local television news reports and in the papers. With a full stock of buggies in the store and burgeoning community goodwill, sales would explode. And in no time, they would be summoning Mr. Crumpler to the corporate office to offer him the helm of the newest, biggest Red Food Store or perhaps even elevate him to District Manager.

Dwight P. Crumpler, they would surely say, is a man who knows how to turn lemons into lemonade.

A FEW DAYS later a Red Food truck lumbered up to the Towers, bearing the donations. The special gift buggies had been helpfully spray-painted bright red to distinguish them from the silver ones belonging to the store. As the buggies were unloaded, the residents looked on warily, suspecting they were being conned in some manner without quite being able to put a finger on it.

But as the store's purloined buggies were rounded up and loaded for return to #100, the residents were reassured this was all happening simply and solely because Red Food cared about them and wanted to reward them for their business.

Mr. Crumpler spent all of two days basking in the glow of his solution. And then, the old pattern reasserted itself as store buggies began to disappear again. To his dismay, Mr. Crumpler found the Towers residents were not using the gift buggies. The few that had been spotted had been abandoned haphazardly along sidewalks near the Towers. The seniors had reacted to the gift of the red buggies as if they had been given warm jars of sputum—something they already had in abundance.

The reasons for this were not difficult to work out. For one thing, the buggies were ugly, having been spray painted. Also— and this was probably a more salient point—the buggies did not roll. They had been retired for a reason, which is that not one of them had a full set of functioning wheels. When you pushed one of these charity buggies it would move—if it moved at all— in a direction other than the one you intended to go, and it did so with great fanfare, squeaking and grinding all the way. Advancing in any kind of straight line required superhuman strength, which no one residing in the Towers possessed. Add to that the element of gravity—negotiating the hill involved in the trip—and there was no way any senior citizen was going to use a red gift buggy.

In short order, Red Food Store #100 was out of buggies again. Mr. Crumpler knew this would be inexplicable and inexcusable to his boss at corporate who had helped him engineer this brilliant solution.

He had only one option, and it was fraught with risk. He had to send Boyd back up the hill for retrieval of his buggies. Shrewdly, he waited until early afternoon when most of the retirees were sure to be napping.

Down the hill came Boyd, again, with an impressive train of buggies. This time he had cajoled a custodian into unlocking the storage room where many of them were secreted away. He had almost all of them.

Mr. Crumpler was so elated he couldn't limit himself to a single interjection. GREAT! GREAT! GREAT!

Boyd beamed with this unprecedented affirmation, but even in the moment of triumph, a mighty wave of fury was building at the Towers. They were already enraged, having discovered the red gift buggies were unusable relics, and now as word spread that the functional buggies—*their* buggies—had been confiscated, the old timers began to coalesce as a mighty force against Mr. Crumpler. Here was a man whose true mission in life, to persecute the city's most vulnerable citizens, had just been revealed. They had loyally shopped at his store, given him their business and now they had been tricked.

It was outrageous, wrong, cruel, intolerable.

And it would not stand. The people of the Towers were timid and vulnerable in many respects, but this was a situation they knew how to handle. Within minutes they were working the phones en masse, complaining bitterly about how Red Food did not want them to shop at its store.

They called the Chattanooga Times. And the Chattanooga

News-Free Press. And Channel 9. And WDEF Radio. And the Better Business Bureau.

A few of the seniors who had expansive views of what constituted an emergency even called the police and fire department.

Worse than all that, the phone lines were clogged at Red Food corporate headquarters. One craggy voice after another demanding to speak to whoever was in charge of Red Food, immediately if not sooner.

Prior to this moment, it is doubtful the company president had spent more than five seconds of his life thinking about Store #100. Perhaps in some vague recess of his mind he knew it was where they sent employees they wanted to punish, but it was not a store that ever warranted any of his attention or concern. Now, suddenly, he was faced with a public relations imbroglio that threatened the reputation of the entire chain. He didn't know exactly what was going on but divined enough from the angry calls to know some idiot manager at his most irrelevant store had just put the entire tri-state operation in jeopardy.

———

AT THIS TIME Mr. Crumpler was sitting in his office—an elevated, open-topped booth overlooking the checkout lanes which gave him a commanding view of the store. He was punching away happily at an adding machine, utterly unaware that his actions of the last hour had just well and truly shredded his career aspirations.

Boyd was wiping sweat from his brow, regaling me with his account of the second great buggy repossession, when the phone rang in the booth. I glanced over to see Mr. Crumpler lift the receiver and assault the caller with his usual earsplitting greeting. For a moment he continued making calculations with his free hand until he realized the boss of all bosses was on the other end. And then he stopped cold, his chubby fingers suspended above the adding machine.

Yes sir.

Yes sir, I did.

Well, because they had all our buggies, and we didn't have–

Umm ... yes sir.

But I—

At this juncture, Mr. Crumpler went all Casper-like as the blood drained from his face. He was silent for a long period as the caller unloaded. This was one interaction he would not be able to crush with optimism.

Yes sir, he said, one more time, his voice faltering.

No goodbyes were exchanged. Ever so gently—almost as if he were handling an explosive—Mr. Crumpler carefully replaced the receiver.

He sat for a minute or two wearing a thousand-yard stare.

Then he stood and called out for his head bagboy, not only yelling in a voice infused with panic but waving him over frantically.

BOYD, Mr. Crumpler said, TAKE SOME OF THEM BUGGIES BACK UP TO THEM OLD PEOPLE AT THE TOWERS, MAKE IT QUICK.

Boyd—still exhausted from the last run—could scarcely believe what he had heard. His red bow tie was hanging limply by a solitary clip, and he was flapping the collar of his shirt, trying to force air down into his chest. For a moment, his aura of courteousness dissolved.

Say what?

YOU HEARD ME, Crumpler bellowed, and now he was shaking. TAKE SOME BUGGIES AND GIT UP THERE RIGHT THIS SECOND!

Mr. Crumpler never spoke to me of his exchange with the president of Red Food, but the outline of the conversation filtered through later from other sources. The call included an ultimatum that if buggies were not returned to the Towers within five minutes, Mr. Crumpler was to be terminated forthwith. The President also threw in a few gratuitous comments about Crumpler's lineage and ineptitude, positing further that he was unquestionably the dumbest manager in the long history of Red Food.

Crumpler survived the immediate aftermath, but the fire had gone out of him, and he was never the same. He still said GREAT! when asked how he was, but it had a hollow, inauthentic ring to it. His meetings were no longer pep rallies but muted, depressing affairs. Sometimes, the words barely trickled from his lips, nearly inaudible.

A few months later, I arrived at work one day to find the beleaguered Mr. Crumpler was no longer the manager of Red Food Store #100. An array of stories was bruited about regarding his departure, but everyone knew that it was the old people and the buggies that had done him in.

By now he would be retired. The Red Food benefits program was never very good. I hope he did not have to move to the Towers.

## Chapter 25

## *The TV Dinner*

I was haunted by the Swanson's turkey dinner, all the way from Chattanooga to Phoenix, 1,765 miles. Peas. Gravy, they claimed. Stuffing. Mashed potatoes. Something masquerading as cranberry sauce, and the turkey. All transformed to ice-brick solid, maybe years earlier, neatly compartmentalized in the plastic tray, ready for the microwave.

I couldn't shake the grim thoughts about that turkey dinner, up through Tennessee, across Arkansas, Oklahoma, the Texas Panhandle, New Mexico and down the spine of Arizona.

---

The Swanson's turkey dinner had been brought to my attention the year before, at Red Food Store #100. It was the Wednesday before Thanksgiving, and we were besieged by the inevitable wave of customers and their last minute clamoring for the ingredients they lacked to assemble the next day's grand feast.

And then the stringy-haired guy ambled in and asked me if I would direct him to the section with the TV dinners.

Sure, I can help you with that, I said. I walked him to the frozen aisle.

He was amiable and engaged me in a conversation on the way over. I asked him what he was doing for Thanksgiving. He reached into the cooler.

I'm having this here Swanson's turkey dinner for Thanksgiving, he said.

No, I replied. Tell me you're not.

Yep, he said. I'm going to heat this up, eat it by myself, and watch the Cowboys-Eagles game.

Family? I asked. Friends?

Nope, he answered. Just me. And Swanson's and John Madden and Pat Summerall. He waved cheerfully and left for the register. The smile, I saw, looked slightly artificial and it evaporated as he left. He cut a lonely figure walking out into the twilight.

How sad, I thought, and then I thought nothing more of it.

---

But now alone on the vast, numbing ribbon of Interstate 40, I remembered the dude and his Swanson's turkey dinner. Now I was going to be the one on my own with no family or friends around.

I was coming off a bad breakup and had decided to move to Phoenix for a fresh start. To find myself. To see if I had the grit to make it on my own. I hit the road in a rented Penske box van and a checking account balance of $1,850. Sufficient, I calculated, to pay a couple month's rent, live on ramen, and then maybe have enough left over to slink back home in disgrace if necessary. This was in October, and suddenly came the thought that I was certain to be by myself for Thanksgiving. I would be the stringy-haired guy reaching into the cooler for a Swanson's.

I found an apartment at a good rate, and hauled my meager positions up the stairs, then sat among the boxes, lonely beyond description. Soon I realized the good rate on the apartment probably had something to do with the fact that most of the other tenants were students at the Motorcycle Mechanics Institute nearby. They did their homework in the middle of the night, which involved testing engines they were rebuilding.

The second day I called to follow up on the job opportunity that had been presented to me—in a phone interview before I left Tennessee—as kind of a sure thing. The position had been cut from the budget while I was in transit.

You didn't come out here counting on this, did you? the HR lady asked.

No, of course not, I replied, trying to subdue the panic welling up.

It seemed beyond doubt I had made a monumental mistake.

———

My first Sunday in Arizona I woke up, tried to stifle the depression, put on a suit, and drove over to the nearest church. A greeter directed me to the singles Sunday School class.

It was the usual salmagundi you would find in such a setting. One or two players, a few misfits, a handful of searchers with the unmistakable whiff of despair about them. Mostly, though, normal and nice and reasonably friendly people.

She arrived late and sat on the far side of the room, about as perfect a creature as I had ever laid eyes on. I only caught a brief glimpse of her porcelain skin, fine features and golden-brown rollicking hair as she walked in. Then I was consigned to stealing side glances now and then, with the class already underway to the strains of a couple of guitarists leading attendees in the chorus *Our God is an Awesome God*. And I was thinking, yes, He might be, if He can arrange for me to make her acquaintance.

Whatever the Sunday School lesson was about, or even if there was one, I cannot recall. I was transfixed on the girl. Over the next hour I pared my optimism, telling myself there wasn't much realistic hope of meeting her—especially after glancing around to see others were watching her. It was bordering on a stalking convention. Lots of competition, and probably some of them had jobs and money, for starters.

The class ended and I hovered around, engaging in perfunctory nice-to-meet-you conversations with others, always with one eye on the girl with the elegant curls and—now I could see more—the alluring smile and angelic face and fizzing personality. And the body, well ...

Unbelievably, she meandered over my way.

I'm Stacey she said, extending a hand confidently.

I introduced myself, I think. The rest of the room promptly faded to a very uninteresting opaque.

Her eyes were impossibly green, and she asked questions with them while concurrently posing audible queries. She had a way of conducting a benevolent interrogation that made me feel glad to be the subject.

I stumbled through a conversation, working desperately hard to conceal my intrigue so as not to frighten her off.

For the next month we maneuvered around each other. We conversed and queried and teased and sparred. Her mind was sharp and aspiring, her sense of humor wicked, her laugh intoxicating. And that she seemed to like me, I was thunderstruck.

I found a job but it suddenly became the most irrelevant

sidebar because every waking moment was consumed with thoughts of Stacey and how she was capturing my heart.

The Sunday before Thanksgiving she asked me what I was doing for the holiday. I stammered something about spending it with friends.

Oh, she said. I was going to invite you to our family's Thanksgiving at my aunt's house, but if you already have plans.

It's nothing I can't cancel, I said.

Good, she said. Be there at two.

---

AUNT BECKY LIVED in an expansive ranch house on the edge of the desert, where the air was clean and crisp. I was there at two on the nose. Stacey was late.

I was ushered into a sea of Stacey's relatives, sans Stacey. They did not treat me special, and within a minute or so it became clear this family's love language involved a lot of good natured but vicious put-downs and endless insults. I was on the receiving end of some of them almost immediately. My kind of people.

Then Stacey arrived. She treated me special.

Aunt Becky had the largest television I had ever seen. John Madden and Pat Summerall, larger than life, were in Texas Stadium. I thought about the stringy-haired man and his Swanson's dinner. By some blessing, some miraculous intervention, that wasn't going to be me after all.

In the next room, a frenetic team of women assembled Thanksgiving dinner, and the aromas wafting over were exquisite. Soon I was gorging on mountains of creamy home-cooked potatoes, oven-cooked turkey and ham, rivers of piping hot gravy, endless stuffing, and corn, and green beans, and pumpkin pies smothered in fresh whipped cream.

The Cowboys were leading the Redskins, and Stacey and I wandered outside, away from the others. The air was still hot but darkness had fallen and the stars were out. The moon was only a waxing crescent. It was bright enough though, and I could make out the emerald in Stacey's eyes. We talked for hours, and dreams converged.

Could I drive you home? I asked.

Sure, she said.

She went back into Aunt Becky's house to tell them she was leaving with me.

I was saved.

I was saved, I just knew it.

# Chapter 26

## *Trying*

It was thrilling, those first months with Stacey as my wife. She didn't mind I only had enough money to take her to San Diego for our honeymoon, or that Red Robin was as close as we ever came to fine dining, or that the business I was starting left us repeatedly dangling near insolvency. She overlooked my many shortcomings, fixed a few of my quirks and graciously bore the ones she couldn't. She saw potential in me I didn't see myself.

On top of that it didn't hurt that Stacey was effectively a personal chef of the first order. She worked as hard as I did, yet every night I would arrive home to prodigious meals and stupendous desserts. Life had never been sweeter.

---

In her teen years her family doctor had suggested Stacey might have trouble getting pregnant. She had shared this prognosis with me early in our relationship, but I swept it aside as speculation. Physicians get a lot of things wrong and in any event, whatever was supposed to be the problem would surely be no match for my virility.

And then we began trying.

The first month without a result scarcely bears a conversation. The second month, and the third and the fourth, are mildly irritating. By month five, worries take hold. Fear follows soon thereafter and collects momentum with every passing cycle. And then when hope is really at a low ebb, your friends, relatives, and everyone around you begins reproducing like rabbits. Next comes anguish—renewed and enhanced every thirty days.

For two years, the storm gathered. Stacey put on a brave face most of the time, but out of sight of others she crumbled. Cried in the car on her way to work. And from work. Cried in the bathroom. Cried for answers. She wanted to be around pregnant people, even though it pained more.

She bought pregnancy test kits endlessly. That can't be right, she would say, on reading the results. Or, I was certain this time. Or, I know I felt something. Every time, though, negative. Then grief. Negative. Grief. Negative. Grief.

Ovulation predictor kits. And special calendars and charts. I hadn't even known there were such things.

And tracking basal body temperature. I was instructed as to when I was to perform, and the timing had to be precise, a matter of utmost importance and urgency.

Get in here now, she summoned from the bedroom. One such time I tarried over my Nintendo when the order came, inasmuch as I was in the middle of a crucial level in the *Legend of Zelda*.

Be there in a minute, I said.

Never made that mistake again.

She shopped for maternity clothes she longed to soon need. We frequented Babies "R" Us with such regularity I could have walked the aisles blindfolded and never skinned a shin. And everyone, everywhere, it seemed, was pregnant. Now we were in the Sunday School class for young married couples, and eleven out of the fifteen couples were with child.

Every second of every day, Stacey hoped, and tested, and hurt.

———

We were at the mall one night and I had just turned from the counter with my large Orange Julius. The girl who took my money and handed me the drink was pimpled and ungainly and might have been sixteen, and her belly was ready to pop.

Stacey smiled and asked the girl about her pregnancy and when she was due and all that. When we walked away the smile, genuine as it was in that moment, faded quickly.

Just once, said Stacey. For just once in my life, I want to know what it feels like to be pregnant.

She held back the tears until we got in the car, and then we drove home in silence and gloom.

## Chapter 27

### *The Cat*

THERE ARE SOME DAYS WHEN YOU EMBRACE THE IDEA that the Almighty has a plan for you even though things may be going badly, and then there are other days when you can only conclude God flat out hates your guts.

I was fed up with everything on this morning, the misery of infertility topping the list. Second was that I didn't have any money to speak of. Then the third thing, my car broke. I felt like it was enough for one day and didn't know it was all just a prelude to an unimaginably greater horror.

Everyone thinks being your own boss is the greatest thing, but the glory fades quickly if you can't pay the bills. I had been relentlessly scrapping away for months and though we weren't starving, I could never generate quite enough income to get caught up.

We just need a few good days of business, I would say to Stacey, and she would nod sympathetically. She knew a few good days of business would invariably be followed by a few bad days, and we would soon be back in the soup with me lying in bed, staring at the ceiling all night with my heart racing.

When the bad days outweigh the good days, even if only by a slender margin, you soon find yourself working endless hours effectively for nothing. And then soon after that your labors are wholly devoted to supporting the Internal Revenue Service and its warm and caring agents. In my conversations with them it was made crystal clear they wanted first dibs, and it didn't worry them if I didn't have any money left over to buy groceries or make mortgage payments.

And my wife—driving the Beretta GT around town at ever-increasing speeds as her frustration mushroomed—was always a nagging concern. I had taken to perusing her car every evening when I arrived home half expecting to find the remnants of pedestrians lodged in the grill.

---

THINGS HAD GOTTEN heated between me and God that morning, the discussion culminating with me telling Him that frankly, things could not be much worse for us, and I really didn't appreciate the fact we didn't have a baby, and He wasn't sending me any business, evidently content to sit by doing nothing to help while we suffered.

God responded by immediately breaking my car. Literally minutes after I'd aired these unvarnished grievances the engine begin rasping and choking, and I looked in the mirror to see a huge column of black smoke billowing from the tailpipe.

They say God always answers prayers, it's just that sometimes the answer is No. They don't mention that sometimes the *No* is accompanied by a resounding sucker punch to the solar plexus.

I clattered into the nearest service station. Not one I would have chosen but the options had been whittled down to whatever was within coasting distance. The reception area wasn't encouraging, consisting as it did of the fragrance of stale oil, the ubiquitous smudge marks on every surface, a couple of orange molded plastic chairs, and a filthy desk with pressboard showing through on the edges where the laminate had worn off. A tipsy wire rack offered up several packages of Tom's brand cheese crackers, no doubt expired. A dog-eared 1992 Cindy Crawford calendar on the wall, down to its last pushpin, showed evidence of having been scrutinized repeatedly with greasy hands.

I was just beginning to contemplate how this calendar was being utilized for scheduling, given this was 1994, when the proprietor materialized from the service bay.

A cigarette dangled loosely from the bearded face and with a noted dearth of introductory formalities he asked—it was more of a grunt really—what it was that I needed. The man was thoroughly hung over, but his expression brightened when I described the car's symptoms.

Call me when you know what's wrong, I told him.

———

It was about a half-mile from there to my office. Summer in Phoenix, the temperature hadn't bothered to dip below 90 degrees overnight and now the sun was beating down on my head as I began the trek along a busy avenue. I used the extra time to grumble to myself about this latest devilish attack and to pray that whatever had happened to my car would be inexpensive to fix. I knew instinctively it was a futile petition.

Can you make it any worse for me, God? I mean, really.

I'm aware you really shouldn't be using sarcasm with God because you know it could always be worse. But there was an understanding between me and God about saying things couldn't be worse. I knew that He knew things really would be worse if, for example, I was paralyzed, but that specific tragedy was off the table for purposes of our discussion.

I had suffered from a pronounced fear of quadriplegia since age thirteen and naturally it was ESJ's doing. Back then she had purchased the autobiography of Joni Eareckson and demanded I read it. The book was an account of a seventeen-year-old girl who took a dive into shallow water in Chesapeake Bay, broke her neck and was paralyzed from the neck down. Joni tells about the rehab and being stuck in a Stryker frame, suffering all the difficulties of being completely dependent on other people to do everything, up to and including blowing her nose, and how she wanted to kill herself but didn't have any way to do it. It was enormously sad and I cowered in my room as I read it with the door closed where nobody could see me. Then later I pulled myself together, came out and told ESJ the book was boring and stupid.

But Joni's story frightened me and I never forgot it. For years afterward every night when I went to bed, I thanked God I was not paralyzed, and asked Him to help me to never, ever be paralyzed.

So every time I started feeling sorry for myself a little voice inside my head would say, at least you're not paralyzed like Joni.

And if the little voice in my head happened to be taking a break, ESJ would pick up the slack by reminding me, whenever she perceived I wasn't bounding with happiness, to be grateful I wasn't paralyzed, like Joni.

God could do it to you at any time if you don't straighten up, she would warn. And then she would proceed to worry incessantly about being paralyzed herself, on top of all her worrying about getting a brain tumor.

After several years of this, I said to God that we would just have an understanding that whenever I was complaining about something, even if I said things can't get any worse, I knew technically they really could get worse, because I could be paralyzed. Just to keep the prayers to a reasonable length, we would agree I didn't have to specifically mention quadriplegia or paraplegia every time.

---

I WAS NEARLY to the office now, and the sweat was teeming down my back. There was a whiff of something unpleasant and I looked over to the street to see a deceased cat near the curb, portly and ripening in the sun. The poor animal's head was bloated and about three times normal size, and the exposed teeth and unseeing eye leered at me ghoulishly. I've always loved cats and felt a stab of sympathy for him, but then thought about how his suffering was over and he probably never knew what hit him. And furthermore he didn't have to worry today about how much his auto repairs were going to set him back.

This was probably a sign from God I should have been grateful I wasn't a maggot-filled cat, but I was beyond the capacity to care about any other creature. I quickly walked on and returned to wallowing in my own despair.

Back at the office I spent the morning sulking and not getting any new business. The greaseball from the service station called to tell me I would need a new carburetor, which obviously was not in stock and would have to be shipped in tomorrow. And it was going to cost five hundred and something dollars.

This is really getting to be outlandish, I thought. A great wave of self-pity was building and with it, no small amount of resentment.

I called Stacey and asked her to pick me up after work, told her the latest news, whined and complained.

And I'm done praying, I said.

What?

Not forever maybe, but for now. This week, at least. It's not doing any good. Making things worse, in fact.

She was mildly alarmed but didn't have the energy to battle my instant conversion to agnosticism, and probably anticipated it would pass.

Well, she said, I don't think I'd be going around saying things can't get any worse. They can always get worse.

Right, I responded. I suppose I could be vaporized by a meteor, although that might not actually be worse.

She sighed and hung up.

I had always derived a certain amount of gratification from moping but others in my presence seemed to find it unpalatable. With even my wife unwilling to share in my misery, I had nothing left to do but go to lunch.

It would need to be somewhere within walking distance, and somewhere cheap. There was a submarine sandwich shop back up the street, near the service station. Two-dollar meatball subs. It would have to do. I rounded up a handful of quarters and ventured back out into the searing air.

---

It was even hotter now, and the waves of heat rising from the sidewalk combined with the sun to create an inferno. My head was down in defeat as I focused all thoughts around my sad predicament.

Thanks for everything, God, and I appreciate the added touch of letting me experience all this persecution in an oven.

Steps developed into a tempo as I watched the seams in the sidewalk pass under my feet and I fell into a grim trance. One, two, three steps, seam, one, two, three steps, seam, one, two, three steps, seam. And with the rhythm came the words:

My, life, stinks, seam, my, life, stinks, seam, my, life, stinks.

Shoulders drooping, angry, confused, bitter. I knew I was being ridiculous but didn't want to stop. Then the little voice in my head interrupted: it could always be worse. Maybe it was my voice, or Stacey's, or God's. It was somebody's. Among all the traffic whizzing by, I heard the groaning diesel of an approaching truck. I didn't look up, didn't want to lose the cadence.

My, life, stinks, seam.

There was a great succulent pop, like a watermelon bursting, and then suddenly I was wet, having walked into a swirling, warm, mysterious red mist. It was a fine mist, but with chunks.

The first sensation was a loss of vision. My right eye had gone dark. Dear God, was it a stroke? Maybe He had it in for me and was going to put me in a wheelchair with a stroke. I would be paralyzed worse than Joni. He was going to freeze my mind, too.

I sent a mental transmission down to the arms, ordering them up, not knowing if they would respond. My hands appeared in front of my face. Upper extremities still working, praise Jesus, maybe it wasn't a stroke. But what was all over my arms?

And I was still walking. One, two, three. Forget the seams, couldn't see them anyway.

Ten more steps, walking in wonderment, and finally—finally—I realized what had happened, and it was going to be more than I could abide. The passing truck, the dead cat—this was about where I had seen it earlier on my way to the office. I stopped and turned and looked back to the curb.

The truck had barreled over the rotting cat at the precise

moment I was next to it on the sidewalk. Like a grenade, the poor creature's head had exploded, showering me with putrescent blood and flesh. I soon discovered I was not blind, but rather a great glob of cat brain had lodged on one of the lenses of my glasses, obscuring my vision. There were pieces of cat pulp in my hair, on my shoes, on my ear, in my mouth. And a great stinking bloody wet mess mottled my shirt and pants.

Suddenly overcome with nausea, I reeled to the edge of the sidewalk and retched.

Now, the acquisition of a meatball sub was no longer among my interests.

I ran back to the office at a full sprint. The sensible thing to do would have been to go home at once, soak in a vat of disinfectant and burn the clothes, but such an option would be available only to someone with access to transportation.

The rest of the afternoon was invested in wiping away liquefied feline, gargling, and cursing the day of my birth. And bits of the cat kept materializing. I would return from the bathroom thinking it was cleaned up, and here I would discover a little blood spatter on my sleeve. Or a piece of tissue behind an ear lobe. And there, a tiny nugget of brain matter on my heel I somehow missed. And always, the dreadful taste of decayed cat in my mouth. It went on all day, and with every new discovery, the little voice was saying

I told you it could be worse.

At five thirty Stacey picked me up. I'm sorry about the carburetor she said, as I shut the door.

The what?

The carburetor.

Oh, right. Almost forgot about that.

She glanced over, puzzled. How could you forget about it? You said it was the worst thing ever.

It thought it was, I replied, but it wasn't.

# Chapter 28

## *Amwaylaid*

Do you ever feel like you could use a little extra money? he asked, looking at me hopefully.

Dear Lord, I thought. Not again.

This was the question you got when you owned a business and went to church and, I suppose, were endowed with a countenance of extreme gullibility: A parade of Amway Independent Distributors at your doorstep, thick with fantasies of assimilating your client base into their downline. Regular as clockwork they came in, sans appointment, eager to share the incredible opportunity.

This is truly a once in a lifetime chance to get in on the ground floor, they would say.

Or: You owe it to yourself to check this out.

Or: I knew you would be interested in this because you're such a smart businessman.

Or my favorite: God told me to share this with you.

They were carefully coached not to mention the company name—for they at least recognized it was universally laden with scorn—but the absurd and unvarying talking points gave them away every time. That, and the patented technique of exploiting relationships at church to recruit business.

The most rabid were the ones just returned from an Amway convention where they had been plied with tales of renovated riffraff who were now paying cash for Rolls Royce Phantoms and Hawaiian vacation estates after discovering the miracle of network marketing. It's not easy to shake off someone who's been pumped up and immunized against common sense and programmed to ignore even the most hostile rejection, and that's what I was up against when Dwayne came at me with the question about making more money.

Simply saying I wasn't interested would bounce off him without effect, so I tried a reply he wouldn't have been trained to answer.

I've really got all the money I need, I said. Anything more would ruin me.

He laughed, but then saw I was somber faced. Dwayne didn't know what to make of my deadpan response, because he didn't know me much at all. He had only recently taken an interest in my spiritual and financial life after his attendance at the Amway conference.

Well anyway, he said, regrouping, Kelli and I would really like to sit down with you and Stacey to have dinner, just to get to know you better.

I did not want to have dinner with Dwayne or his wife Kelli. I knew it was a ploy, and I knew he wanted to get to know us better only to the extent we could be a cog in his imaginary multilevel empire. Besides, I didn't like Dwayne, even before this. He was a squirrelly, flatulent little pretend hippy, balding on top with a buffoonish ponytail he stroked constantly, as if it were a pet.

Yeah, we would love to have dinner, I said. I'll look at my schedule and get back to you. Been really busy, though.

The moment it came out of my mouth, I knew it was a mistake—suggesting I was busy. My intent was to transmit, without subtlety, a profound lack of interest in having dinner or meeting him anywhere at any time. But Dwayne heard a trigger word he'd been trained to pounce on. The beady eyes darted around for a moment and the lip quivered in excitement as he realized the opening had been presented.

Well, I've got some really exciting information, he said feverishly. Even if you are doing okay financially, this is something to help you with the busyness. You know, give you more free time to spend with your family. Kelli and I would love to share it with you and Stacey, because it's been a real answer to prayer in our lives.

I'm not interested in Amway, I said flatly. I've heard all about it, many times.

Aggrieved, Dwayne stuttered for a moment and took a step back.

I didn't say it was Amway, he replied.

Yeah, but it is, isn't it?

There was a pause as Dwayne's mind thrashed out ways to regain control of the conversation. Somewhere in his head, a little voice was parroting the admonition they had pounded into him: whatever you do ... no matter what ... don't tell them it's Amway.

I'll give you the details about it later, he said with a defensive wave of the hand. It really is something that will change your life, I promise. A real blessing from the Lord.

I cringed. There it was again, bringing God into the proposal. My discussions with the Lord these days mostly involved asking Him to get us a baby, and I wasn't getting much of a response. If Dwayne was to be believed, God was currently now focusing his attention on Amway Independent Distributors rather than procreation. It was grotesquely offensive.

SEVERAL WEEKS WENT by with Dwayne making futile entreaties which mostly involved invitations to this or that restaurant. I knew from experience when Amway distributors invite you to dinner, it does not mean they actually intend to pay for your dinner. They won't. You will sit there in misery for hours listening to fantastical projections of imminent wealth and then, at the end of it all, they will scheme to avoid the check. This is because they've emptied their savings account to buy three thousand rolls of Amway toilet paper which are rotting in the garage, and they are broke.

Many explicit rejections later there was a lull, and I thought Dwayne had just about packed it in and moved on to other marks. But then we received a call one evening just as Stacey was pulling spaghetti off the stove.

This is Dwayne, said the voice on the line. Kelli and I are in the neighborhood. Can we stop in?

Well, we were just getting ready to have dinner, I said.

Oh, that's perfect, he replied. We haven't eaten yet. He hung up before I could respond.

Less than a minute later, they were at the door. I begrudgingly ushered them in as Stacey added a couple of plates to the table. Somewhere in the back of my mind was a faint memory of a biblical command about showing hospitality to people because you never know when you might be entertaining angels. But I wasn't happy about it, and my mood didn't improve any when Dwayne began spooning vast mounds of my spaghetti onto his dish.

I knew an Amway presentation was forthcoming and as Dwayne and Kelli gorged themselves, a growing sense of indignation was welling up inside.

Dwayne took a napkin and wiped it across his mouth, and then only partially stifled a burp.

I want to ask you a simple question, he said. Would you guys be willing to pay a little more for better quality products?

No, I replied. And anyway, when you allege your products are better quality, you are assuming facts not in evidence.

Dwayne couldn't process that answer, but fortunately he had his secret weapon, Kelli, to step in and take over the case. She turned to Stacey and proceeded, in so many words, to lecture her on how she was wasting money by shopping at retail grocery stores.

No doubt the experts at the Amway conference had prescribed this approach. Make your appeal directly to the woman. She makes the household purchases.

There were two enormous problems with this strategy, as Dwayne and Kelli were about to discover. The first was that Stacey was an unequaled genius when it came to saving money. She had a sophisticated scheme of shopping, honed over many years, which combined an encyclopedic knowledge of store sales patterns with a trove of coupons, expertly organized. Ask her where to buy, say, a box of Fruit Loops, and Stacey would instantaneously retrieve the coupon from a file of hundreds and tell you which store to visit and when. The Dewey Decimal System was rudimentary and quaint in comparison. It wasn't uncommon for Stacey to come out of a store with bags full of groceries having not paid a dime.

―――

KELLI'S CLAIM that Stacey was overspending on groceries was sheer lunacy, only Kelli didn't know it yet. But it was about to get worse, because she followed up with an ill-fated remark that doomed the presentation and accelerated the supper self-invitation to a tempestuous conclusion.

One of the great things about this program, Kelli chattered on naively, is it takes away so much worry. You have a lot going on in your life, and I know that once you start saving money with this—and making money—you'll be able to relax more and the Lord will free you from a lot of your stress and problems.

Did I really just hear that? I thought to myself.

These vultures had attended our Sunday School class, listened to our prayer requests about wanting a baby, and perceived it as an opening to get us in their downline. And Kelli had just taken the oldest, most offensive, most ignorant canard anyone can ever say to someone suffering through infertility and packaged it in an Amway presentation.

It was not the first time someone had suggested we would have a baby once we just quit worrying about it and relaxed, but the notion that a home-based network marketing business would also be required was certainly original.

I had a catalog of distasteful retorts percolating, but I was not going to need any of them now because Stacey was incandescent with rage.

I've heard it said you should choose your words carefully when speaking to a pregnant woman. I don't know if that's true, but I am well informed you should tread lightly around a woman who has been trying unsuccessfully to have a baby for a long time. Telling her it's all in her head is not advisable.

You don't know what you're talking about, said Stacey, the comment accented with a forefinger jabbed toward Kelli's face.

Oh yes, I do, Kelli replied.

There followed a couple of hostile exchanges, but I don't remember the precise statements because my attention was focused on restraining Stacey, who was now rising from her chair. Across from me Dwayne was tugging anxiously at his wife's sleeve, a look of wild terror in his eye. Kelli seemed not to appreciate what was unfolding. I didn't know exactly what would happen if I released my grip on Stacey, but there was every indication she was ready to launch across the table like a rocket. I knew if her hands got around Kelli's throat they wouldn't be coming off until the police arrived. I certainly wouldn't be able to pry them away, and Dwayne and his wimpy ponytail would be useless.

It's time to go, he said, voice infused with rising panic. It's time to go. It's really time to go.

Finally, Kelli began to comprehend the peril. They scooted back from the table and headed for the door, Dwayne pulling at her with desperate enthusiasm. Even if we'd wanted to say goodbye, they were in their car and down the street before we had a chance. We never heard from Dwayne and Kelli about Amway again. In fact, we never really talked to them afterwards, as they seemed to make a point of maintaining a buffer zone of one hundred feet or so between us at church.

Eventually, I was told, the couple lost several thousand dollars and alienated all their friends and loved ones. They left Amway and resumed the pursuit of their entrepreneurial dreams with Herbalife. But the Lord presumably did not reveal to Dwayne and Kelli any need on our part for vitamins or aloe products.

# Chapter 29

## *The Deal*

I WAS IMMENSELY PLEASED ABOUT THE DEAL.

It was an achievement to get my wife to postpone plans of getting a baby when it was the only thing she ever wanted. I was delighted with myself and rightfully so, but now I had to do something. It was October and under the specific terms of the Deal I had until the first of January to come up with some sort of plan. After that she would be rampant.

At five o'clock on the morning after the Deal was secured, I rolled out of bed and shuffled to the spare room back in the corner of the house. It was slated to be the bedroom for child number two someday, but right now was a stockpile of infant paraphernalia, purchased in anticipation of a baby, along with all manner of books and picture frames and boxes and out-of-season clothes and other junk.

There was a rolltop desk in the corner somewhere under all that. I forged a path over to it, repositioned some of the oddments, rolled up the cover and found a pad of paper on which I neatly wrote down my pressing prayer requests:

1. Money

2\. Baby

It was time to have a pointed conversation with God. Or the voice in my head. Or someone. I was never quite confident who was speaking to me because I had a vivid lifelong practice of talking to myself without ever being entirely sure if the responses I was hearing came from God, Satan, Satan's minions, or just the voice in my head. Maybe this time it would be obvious.

The plan was to pray about these items of concern with enhanced enthusiasm which would stimulate God to recognize I had reached my Moses in the wilderness moment. He would reveal a magical solution posthaste in the form of some affluent new clients who would rain down mammon. God would understand, of course, that His answers had to be delivered in the order presented on my sheet, because you can't get a baby without a lot of money. Something between ten and twenty five thousand dollars would be the place to start, that being what you usually had to pay an attorney and adoption agency to get things in motion. I had no hope of getting this money on my own, but the Almighty could come up with something, if He would only listen for once.

There was no chair and so I sat on the floor among all the detritus and prayed vigorously for some time and then read some psalms and then prayed some more, and then I listened carefully for some direction. Nothing happened and it was soon evident that God was taking the day off.

The only thing popping into my mind—and it seemed preposterous and irrelevant and surely not from the heavenly realms—was an absurd old BBC children's show I hadn't thought about in many years, probably since the last time I saw it. For some reason it blotted out all my attempts at lofty spiritual meditation.

*Jim'll Fix It*, was the name of the show. The host was Jimmy

Savile, a shady looking character with flowing white hair and big, ugly shutter-sized teeth and a creepy laugh who was supposedly a great, magical benefactor. His program featured mostly British schoolchildren who would write in, expressing some wish, and Jim would read the letter on the telecast and then go about granting their wish. At the end of the show the children whose wish had been fulfilled by Jim were draped with immense, gaudy medals that said *Jim Fixed It for Me*. The studio audience would clap and cheer in utter transport while the children beamed at having their wishes granted.

It was intriguing at first but then after watching a few episodes I began to realize Jim wasn't a magician of unlimited means, but was quite plainly working within the strict confines of the BBC's spartan government budget. Nobody ever seemed to get on the show with any really grand dreams, like going to Disneyland or swimming in the Great Barrier Reef or going anywhere involving a substantial plane fare. If you wanted to go to the World Cup in Argentina, Jim wasn't going to fix that for you. If your grandmum had cancer and needed special treatment, you would not be hearing back from Jim.

The winners, such as they were, involved people with strictly pedestrian-level dreams like being the drummer for a day with the Boomtown Rats, or working as a train engineer on the London to Liverpool run, or attending a live taping of the *Benny Hill show*, or visiting the beach at Brighton, or meeting a certain football player, or having a sandwich at the local pub named after a favorite uncle who had been gassed in the war.

*Jim'll Fix It*. That is all that came into my head the first day of the great prayer crusade to get a baby.

---

I WENT TO WORK. Nothing much happened out of the ordinary, no big money clients. I returned home to a morose wife and got up the next morning and went to the spare room again and looked at my list again and prayed again.

Some guidance would be nice, God. I'm humbled. I really am. Need some money. How do you want me to get it?

Nothing.

Well, not literally nothing. *Jim'll Fix It* came to my mind again. I'm not very good at meditating, I thought. I need to go deeper.

The next day I got up earlier and tottered bleary-eyed back to the rolltop. I concentrated more. I prayed longer and threw in a couple of proverbs and read the biblical story of Joseph—he had a few bad breaks—and waited expectantly for my answers.

Again there was only Jimmy swimming around in my head with the garish grin and the outlandish cheesiness.

Not a word of Heavenly comfort, no ideas about making more money, no answers, no hope.

You know, God, I said, adopting a more informal tone while adding a touch of belligerence, you are being stunningly silent.

Again all I heard in reply was *Jim'll Fix It, Jim'll Fix It, Jim'll Fix It.*

Presumably this was the voice in my head, not God, but just on the off-chance it was God who kept bringing him up, I thought I should respond.

Jimmy was a fraud, I blurted out in my head. I'm at the end of my rope with this, and all you have is *Jim'll Fix It*? He didn't really fix anything, you know, unless you had something cheap and easy to fix. You didn't get on the show if you had any serious problems or any big dreams. It was all small-potato, stupid stuff. My issue here is substantial. I mean, your biggest dream in life is to meet the Boomtown Rats? Seriously?

Jimmy was a fraud, I said again, louder. Jimmy couldn't fix anything real.

I know, said God, or the voice in my head. And neither can you.

And then I remembered what Stacey had said to me, just a few days earlier but forgotten in a haze of grief.

You can't fix this, she had said.

And I realized, now, that it was true. Jim'll Fix It, the BBC one, was a charlatan. And Jim'll Fix It, the undersigned, had no more hope of granting this wish.

God and the voice in my head and Stacey, they were all saying the same thing.

What do you want me to do? I asked whoever was listening.

Crickets.

What do you want me to do? I asked again. We need money. I have a deadline here.

You don't get it, said God or the voice in my head. It's not up to you. You can't fix this. You can't fix anything.

Then the voice got louder, and clearer, and more emphatic.

*You.*

*Can't.*

*Fix.*

*Anything.*

Doom wrapped itself around me.

I placed my paper back in the desk and lowered the lid and went to work. The entire conversation had been entirely unsatisfactory, and I was still undecided as to whether I was hearing from God or taking leave of my senses.

But it never went away, the message. You can't fix this.

It followed me to work and back home.

---

I GOT to the house before Stacey. All alone, I went back to the corner office. The blinds were closed, and it was somber and cool. I stood in the pile of rubbish and looked around. The roll-top, with its ham-fisted two-item list of prayer demands tucked inside, remained closed. I didn't feel strong enough to open it.

You can't fix this, God said.

Pretty sure it was Him this time. He hadn't even waited for me to repeat the question.

Ok, I said. I hear you.

# Chapter 30

## *The Miser*

SHE SPENT LITTLE ON PERSONAL COMFORTS, WAS THE WAY they wrote it.

They being the people at the *World Book* encyclopedia. It was just a short entry, and they didn't say anything about how everyone hated her or how she had bad teeth and was attended by a dumpsteresque aroma. And how she was crazy, though maybe like a fox.

She spent little on personal comforts. Considerable understatement.

———

I WAS a kid in England reading about Hetty Green because it was raining out. The only thing on the BBC was a torpid documentary program called *Panorama*, and I was driven to the *World Book* as a higher level of entertainment. People who would not believe the *World Book* can be entertaining have never tried to watch *Panorama*.

Hetty Green, the Witch of Wall Street.

Also, the richest woman in the world. And the meanest. She was the one who spent little on personal comforts. World record miser.

Worth one hundred million dollars in her day, like two billion in today's money, and enjoyed none of it, because she didn't use it for anything beneficial.

Certainly wouldn't let any money go for clothing. Hetty wore the same dress for decades, long after it was all patches and tatters.

Not for her son. Poor old Ned suffered a leg injury after wiping out on his sled. It needed a doctor. He didn't get one. Doctors required payment, which Hetty was unwilling to tender. So gangrene set in eventually, and the boy's leg had to be amputated.

Not for a spouse. She jettisoned her husband when his financial acumen proved to be inferior to her own.

Not for living quarters. She worked on Wall Street but lived in Hoboken, where in the late nineteenth century you could get a dirt cheap, cold water flat and routinely stiff the landlord. That it was rat-infested was beside the point.

Not for friends. She didn't have any.

Hetty was in truth an economic genius, shrewd and cunning and cutthroat, and she outmaneuvered businessmen all over the country at a time when women didn't get anything like a fair shake.

But think of it. Living like you had nothing when you had so much. The richest woman in the world, living down by the docks in Hoboken, in rags.

She died at age 81, finally done in by the anger and bitterness. Reporters followed her and biographers combed through her life, but there's no record of a single act of charity attributable to the Witch of Wall Street. She still had all her money on the day she stroked out. Mission accomplished.

But then much of what she left went to Ned, the son with the cork prosthesis. The money she had saved, he frittered away. Goofball science experiments. Stamp collections. Preposterous parties. Elaborate boats. High dollar prostitutes. Mansions. Gifts of gold coins to random people on the street.

This is your legacy when you won't let go. Someone else lets it go for you.

John Rockefeller built a hospital. Andrew Carnegie built a Hall. Cornelius Vanderbilt, a university. Robber barons maybe, but at least they did something. Hetty Green had all the financial savvy of the great titans of American industry—maybe more—but there's a reason you've probably never heard of her.

She kept everything. She kept everything but then her fortune was boinked away by her one-legged son.

I showed my dad the *World Book* article about Hetty. He liked it. He is a master storyteller. That'll make a great sermon illustration, he said. And that was the last I heard of it for twenty years. But he remembers things.

———

DAD CALLED me one day after we told him about the Doctor. He asked how we were doing.

We're practically broke, I replied, and we're never going to be parents, so not all that good. We're shattered, to be accurate.

My dad prayed for us over the phone.

And then inexplicably, he brought up that long-forgotten entry from the *World Book*. Who was the woman, he asked, from the encyclopedia you told me about one time? The woman who was so rich but lived so poor?

The Witch of Wall Street, I said. Hetty something.

Right, he said. She lived in rags and went around acting like she had nothing, but in reality she had more than anybody?

OK, I said. Whatever.

Well, my dad said, you might have something to learn from the Witch of Wall Street.

Is this a sermon illustration? I asked. I'm not sure I'm in the mood.

The thing is, Dad continued, you're not poor. It's not hopeless. I know you feel that. And my heart's with you, but it's not true. You have an asset to bring to bear on this problem.

What's that? I asked.

But God, he said.

What do you mean, But God? I asked. That's not even a sentence, Dad.

But God, he repeated.

That doctor visit is not the end of the story, he explained. That's just the end of the chapter. Now you turn it over to God and see what His plan is and see what He will do. Think of all the stories of people in scripture who were hopeless, and then the next verse begins, But God.

OK, Dad, I said, I will check it out.

I hung up, and Stacey and I went into the office. We grabbed the floppy disk with the searchable Bible on it and fired up the computer. Turned out the Bible is riddled with *But Gods*.

But God remembered. But God has seen my hardship. But God will be with you.

But God will lead you out. But God intended it for good. But God will surely come to your aid. But God will never forget the needy. But God will redeem you. But God, But God, But God. There were so many we got tired of reading them.

Dad might have something here, I said.

The next morning I returned to the rolltop. I took out my list and looked at it again.

1. Money

2. Baby

Every atom of my being told me this list was complete, and all that was needed was for the Almighty to take a moment out of His day to tackle it in the order presented. But I dutifully reached for my pen and wrote

3. But God.

I didn't feel much of anything, but somehow the list looked better.

# Chapter 31

## *The Pastor*

A FEW PEOPLE SAID WE SHOULD VISIT OUR PASTOR AND tell him about our situation and solicit his prayers. Maybe God is waiting for you to see the preacher, they said, to have him lay hands on you, like Jesus did to heal the sick.

His name was Don Engram. He looked more like an Iowa farmer than a preacher, with the receding hairline and the weathered Romanesque nose and ruddy complexion. But he was a kind and deeply spiritual man possessed of a substantial amount of godliness, and no doubt his prayers would be better than mine. All indications were his petitions went laser-like directly to heaven while mine rarely got out of the rolltop.

Still, I was too beaten down to expect Pastor Don to offer anything miraculous. Maybe though, having his prayers involved would lend a measure of gravitas and, at least, help me in managing the Deal. We need to be patient, I could tell Stacey. The pastor is praying for us. We just need to wait things out for a while.

---

We were ushered into his office which felt like some kind of hallowed sanctuary, with his Bible sitting open on a grand desk and his hundreds of theological books eloquently lining the walls, the plush chairs and unmistakable air of reverence. He waved us over to a sofa, sat down across a coffee table and asked how he could help.

We went through the whole story and chronicled, exhaustively, the pilgrimage of hopelessness. The pastor listened for a long time and then he spoke softly and with compassion. He seemed oddly unperturbed by the firmness of the infertility diagnosis. I had a slight sense he knew something he wasn't saying.

At least he didn't come right out and say we were done, which was nice.

Do you think this situation is too hard for God, he asked?

Seems to be, I thought to myself cynically. But I answered: No, of course not.

Then I saw Stacey, beside me, was demolished. She had reached some critical juncture in her spirit. Inside, I could tell, she was having her own *Jim'll Fix It*-type battle, and a long time later I learned why. She had secretly breached the terms of the Deal, running around asking everyone within earshot if they knew of anyone, anywhere, who had a baby to adopt. I was practically the only one unaware of this, because she had done a masterful job of pretending to adhere to the Deal while in my vicinity. But on this day in the pastor's study, I knew none of this. I only knew we were out of options.

I will pray with you, said pastor Engram, but you have to make a promise.

OK, we answered, inquiringly.

We are going to take this whole thing and lay it at the feet of Jesus, he said, but when we do, you are going to leave it there.

Leaving it at the feet of Jesus. A simple demand it was, a Christian cliché, a devotional throwaway line, a preacher's platitude, only the pastor knew it wasn't. For us, it really wasn't.

He was asking for everything.

The pastor retrieved his Bible and read the words of Paul from Ephesians. It was about grace and peace and redemption and the mystery of God's will. How we were adopted and chosen by God before the foundation of the world. How we were blameless before Him. I had read it a dozen times before, but this time it sounded different. The detritus accumulated over years—years of trying to follow rules, and avoid rules, and fix things, pretending, and making some show of Getting Right with God—was swept away in an instant.

He had us kneel on the floor and he put his arms around us and prayed and it was a tender, saintly, innocent, beautiful plea from the depths of his heart. I felt everything breaking apart inside of me and I knew somehow it was as it should be. I didn't want the prayer to end.

At length it came to a close and we stayed there for a while on the carpet, literally without the strength to get up. The pastor was in his seventies, and I should have felt bad he had to help pull us to our feet.

We wiped away the tears and said thank you ever so much and goodbye and we'll see you Sunday.

At least now God would know what we wanted. Even if we didn't know what God wanted. We had done everything we could. It was totally up to Him now.

Let me ask you something, the pastor said casually as he opened the door. Would you be willing to consider adoption?

I didn't answer, not out loud. Why don't you look at how much money is in my checking account, I was thinking, and see if you want to ask that question.

Yes, Stacey said immediately.

The pastor had one more thing to say as we left, with a point of his finger, and his voice was still kindly but now it was also firm.

Remember, he said, at the feet of Jesus.

# Chapter 32

## *The Church Lady*

Stacey was all alone.

I had her pledged to the Deal. Sure, she was making surreptitious inquiries, but she couldn't very well bring it up with me. Then there was the pastor with his *Leave It at the Feet of Jesus* thing. And it was Christmas time. An extra little knife in the heart.

She was committed to singing in the church Christmas musical. Didn't feel like it, but there was no getting out of it now.

The *Festival of Lights* it was called. Massive production. The church went berserk with the holiday lights, tens of thousands of them strung all over the ceiling. And a hired, professional orchestra. Big choir, covering an expansive stage from end to end. Real Bethlehem-style stable animals excreting in the auditorium, the whole works. People who only came to church once a year would come for the *Festival of Lights*. They packed the auditorium for six performances over the course of the week.

Amid this hoopla, before the Friday performance, Stacey

was walking over to the auditorium. She watched a car pull up to the sidewalk, near the nursery. A tiny girl, maybe fourteen, surfaced from the back seat, her baby in the crook of her arm.

God, this isn't fair, Stacey thought.

Couldn't take her eyes off the girl with the baby. A child, with a child. Stacey watched her stride up the sidewalk with her bundle to the church nursery.

The inequity of it was overwhelming.

In that instant—that *what possibly have I done to deserve this* instant—the surfeit of naïve, stupid counsel and well-meaning but moronic yarns arose to confront her. You're too skinny, put on some weight. You're eating too much sugar. Just relax. Try harder. Stop trying and it will happen. Maybe it's not meant to be. Be patient. Stand on your head after sex. Maybe it's God's will. You don't want to bring a kid into this world anyway. Be grateful for what you have. Take a vacation. Get drunk before sex. Did you hear about the woman with the turkey baster? Give it a few years. Sarah in the Bible gave birth at ninety, what's your hurry? Try this, try that, eat this, avoid that, worked for my sister, worked for my aunt, worked for my coworker, worked for my daughter, worked for this woman I read about. You're done, you're done, you're done.

She watched every step until the girl and the baby disappeared through the door.

God, why are you doing this? I want that baby. I need that baby.

Stacey gathered herself, but not really, and walked over to the auditorium. She botched the words to her solo bit in the Festival of Lights. Her opening line was *dashing through the snow*. She sang *deck the halls*. It just came out of nowhere. *Deck the halls* cannot be made to fit properly in the line where *dashing through the snow* goes. The professional orchestra, being made up of professionals, continued playing *Jingle Bells* as per the song sheet. The next soloist was supposed to take over when the song reached *bells on bobtails ring*, but he was wrecked by Stacey before he got started and never recovered.

After the performance, everyone congratulated everyone as if it had gone splendidly.

———

THERE WAS a guy in the choir named Jeff. It was a big choir, as stated, and Stacey didn't really know him.

A friend pointed him out. That guy over there, Jeff, the friend said to Stacey, gesturing toward the back row. That guy and his wife Karen, they help teen girls who are pregnant. They do whatever is needed. If they need a place to stay, need financial help, interested in adoption, whatever, they help.

Stacey introduced herself to Jeff. I hear you can get me a baby, she said.

He was no doubt taken aback by the distinct lack of subtlety.

Stacey explained who she was and why she was asking. Jeff said, well, maybe you should pray about it.

You don't have any babies now? she asked.

No, he said. We're not like a 7-Eleven where we have them ready to pick out and take to the register. You would need to pray a baby into our home. And call my wife Karen.

Jeff gave Stacey his wife's number.

Stacey didn't call Karen. She wanted to, but there was the Deal. And there was *Leaving It at The Feet of Jesus*. And the heartache of Christmas. When you are lonely and disappointed, Christmas amplifies all the misery.

Saturday night she saw Jeff again. You didn't call, he said.

I've been meaning to, Stacey said. She didn't explain it to him, but there was the Deal. And, *at The Feet of Jesus*.

Sunday night. Jeff asked, are you going to call Karen or not?
I will, Stacey said, I will plan on calling her tonight.

Inside she was thinking, I will call her after Christmas, when the Deal is complete. So she didn't call.

———

ON MONDAY MORNING, six days before Christmas, and the day after the Festival of Lights had mercifully come to an end, Stacey arrived to work early. She was never early, even with the fast car. She always left home late, drove fast, still arrived late. Today, for reasons God only knows, she was early. Nobody else was there. The lights were out.

The phone was ringing. She waited for it to go to voicemail, but it kept ringing

# Chapter 33

## *The Call*

STACEY MADE HER WAY LEISURELY TO THE PHONE, ITS little beige square light beckoning in the darkness. She was in no hurry to answer and hoped the ringing would stop before she got to it. People who call first thing Monday morning are often cantankerous, or aggrieved about something, or both.

Eventually Stacey picked it up and answered professionally, if unenthusiastically.

It was Karen, she of the pray-a-baby-into-our-home plan of adoption, and she had a baby. She had a baby, quite literally in her arms, when she called. Karen, it turned out, was not big on small talk.

I'm holding a baby right now, she said.

In the background Stacey thought she heard little baby noises, but the mind can play heartless tricks when you're this low.

I have a baby, and she's going to be available the day after Christmas. Are you interested?

For a moment, Stacey forgot to breathe, and her heart plunged to the pit of her stomach. And then she remembered the Deal. The day after Christmas was not next year, and the very essence of the Deal was that there would be no more chasing after babies this year. As if to underscore the point, we would be in Tennessee the day after Christmas visiting family anyway. And besides, this isn't how adoption works. Babies are adopted, usually from China or Kyrgyzstan, after all savings accounts have been exhausted. They do not *become available the day after Christmas*, especially when it's December 19. But these were only thoughts, not statements, because Karen had neglected to await an answer to question one and was already delivering question two.

I would like you to come to our house tonight with your husband to talk with us, she said. Can you be here at six?

Tonight? With Jim? Now the impediment of the Deal loomed larger than ever. Stacey could go by herself, perhaps, but the chances of getting me to participate in any baby discussions, in contradiction of the Deal, were uncertain. This was not meant to be. And so Stacey answered woodenly—

Well, we're not going to be here the day after Christmas, we're going to Tennessee.

That would be a problem, said Karen. She was working with several couples interested in adoption, and the timing was important. But undeterred, she forged on.

I want to get to know you anyway, she said. Will you and your husband come tonight?

Stacey fumbled for a moment, trying to explain the Deal to Karen in a benign sort of way, hoping to avoid the inference that she wasn't interested. It didn't seem to make much of an impact on Karen, who repeated her request.

I'm not sure he will, Stacey said, but I will ask.

# Chapter 34

## *The Question*

I kept taking those personality tests and they always said the same thing. I am thinking, not feeling. The first time I took the test it was part of a premarital counseling session. The counselor perused the scores, shook his head in puzzlement, and noted he had never seen anyone so conclusively entrenched in the "thinking" box. He offered no predictions about the likelihood of marital success and was bereft of counsel. However, he felt comfortable I had invested an abundance of logical thought into my choice of mate.

The second examination was an effort by an employer to determine what made his subordinates tick. The theory, as I understand it, was that his employees would work better together if they understood each other's personalities. But what happened, it appeared, was that the test helped the employees understand they didn't like working there. Four left almost at once. But not me. I just kept thinking.

The third test was taken at the behest of another counselor some years into our marriage. He had reviewed my earlier evaluations and demanded a retest. He assumed I had clandestinely submitted test answers compiled by a robot.

So when the call came on December 19, I was thinking, not feeling.

---

I was busy when the call came, and to the extent I am capable of having moods, I was in no mood for it. As a struggling sole proprietor, my work schedule before Christmas was sheer madness as I tried to carve out a few days off so we could enjoy what was our only vacation of the year. I scarcely had time to sleep. Only my brilliant tactic of securing the Deal had enabled me to focus my energy on getting the work fires put out.

But with that phone call, the plan was imperiled. Thanks to the Deal, a thin veneer of calm had glazed over the tumult in our lives. I saw that this proposed meeting threatened to run a rotor-tiller right through the tranquility, and right before Christmas—even though it was presented to me vaguely as an exploratory interview.

I responded with silence.

Then with a calculated and weighty sigh.

And only after I was sure I had fully communicated my unhappiness, I spoke.

Haven't we had enough heartache for now? We promised each other we wouldn't do this. Let's just enjoy Christmas. We need time to regroup. We had a deal.

I knew it wouldn't work.

Please, please do this for me, she said.

---

DARKNESS WAS GATHERING as we walked from the cool desert air and into Karen's house. If ever there was a time for me to be thinking, not feeling, this was it. The Deal may have been scuttled, but I was determined to limit this visit to a minor diversion, and nothing more. We would meet Karen. We would tell her about us. And sometime next year or maybe the year after that, when the timing was right and I somehow had some money, we would get serious about adoption. The task here, tonight, was simply to keep Stacey on an even keel, so we could all sail through Christmas with a modicum of peace.

We were guided into the living room and over to a weathered couch. Stacey sat down exuding—for the moment—a measure of calm, though I thought I detected behind her eyes a potential chain reaction of turmoil building.

Across from us Karen began chattering away about her little ministry to young mothers and listing some of the things she expected of potential adoptive parents. I assumed this to be the preamble to a string of questions, the answers to which would help her gauge whether she would consider us as suitable candidates. So, I was busy thinking – anticipating the forthcoming questions, mentally reviewing the answers I would give that would place us in the proper light as a couple looking to adopt sometime in the future. I wasn't listening intently to what she was saying, but I'd long since mastered the skill of appearing to be at rapt attention even when my mind might be in another zip code.

But as I waited for the questions to begin, something unexpected happened. I became aware the conversation had taken a turn, and Karen seemed to have skipped the expected interrogatories. Now she was talking about a specific baby, and when she finally broke free from the monologue and asked a question, it wasn't one I had prepared for.

Are you ready to see the baby?

For a just a moment longer, I was thinking, not feeling. Had I really heard that? Because nowhere in the itinerary presented to me was the question *are you ready to see the baby* indicated. Is the baby here? Well, I'm not sure if I want to see the baby, I thought.

A wave of uncertainty washed over me. Devoid of baby acquisition experience, my left brain served up the nearest idiom in reach, which was a fundamental rule of negotiation: Avoid the appearance of being overeager. The closest parallel was the process of buying a new car. You take the test drive. You smell the new car smell. You fall in love. The salesman extols the virtues of the rack and pinion steering—which for all you know might be components on the space shuttle—but you nod enthusiastically to convey understanding. You're hooked. And then after a quick mental review you suddenly realize you really can afford a higher monthly payment than you and your spouse discussed before you came in, with only a slight modification to the grocery budget. You'll just eat Ramon noodles for the next sixty months, and after all they come in a variety of flavors. That may be what happens to most car buyers, but not me, because I am thinking, not feeling.

Only this was no dealership. And in its waning moments of dominion, my thinking hemisphere was trying to tell me this surely was not going to work. First, what on earth were we doing here? We didn't know any of these people, and they didn't know us. Their dog was still apprehensive about us, for crying out loud. Why was I being asked if I was ready to see the baby? Well, maybe I was ready to see the baby. And at the very moment I realized the entire thinking process was suffering a colossal meltdown, the answer to *are you ready to see the baby* just came out of my mouth.

Yes, I said.

FROM THE KITCHEN Jeff came forth, holding a something bundled in pink. I couldn't see what was in his arms, but I knew by the way he was holding it, close to his heart, it was precious.

She's sleeping, he said as he gingerly stepped into the arc of light. And then he knelt and passed her ever so softly into Stacey's arms. This is Melanie, he said.

Melanie slept on, utterly undisturbed by the slight jostle of the handoff and knowing nothing of the transfer.

The effect on me was altogether different, for I was certain I was looking upon a very angel from heaven, beautiful and perfect beyond all description. Stricken by adoration I just gazed at her, my thoughts reduced to four simple words, replayed over and over.

She is so beautiful.
She is so beautiful.
She is so beautiful.

From her head, crowned with whispers of golden hair, to the most intricately curled fingers, to impossibly tiny feet encapsulated in shiny white leather, she was so beautiful. I didn't know—or think about—why I was seeing the baby or how any of this could work, but I sensed, overwhelmingly, this was a defining moment of my existence. Abruptly I discovered that breathing had become a laborious, conscious exercise.

Stacey lifted Melanie from her lap and passed her toward me. I cradled my palms to receive her, looking down at my outstretched hands.

These hands were made for this, I thought. As I took Melanie, and she nestled in, I saw that she fit perfectly, just as I already somehow knew she would.

Deep inside, I knew that *Thinking, Not Feeling* was gone

forever, and I was relieved by its departure. The entire philosophy of thinking, not feeling, just now, seemed idiotic.

Through all of this, Karen was still talking, weaving a story muffled by my emotions. I caught bits and pieces, enough to understand I was sitting at the nexus of an unfolding miracle.

The story was that somebody had been watching us, though we didn't know it. We didn't know Katie, Melanie's mother, but she knew us. She had come to our church and watched us from afar. Week after week, she watched Stacey. She watched her sing solos. She watched her in the nursery, and her way with babies. She watched her way with *her* baby. She was watching, all the time. While we withered inside, and doubted, and questioned, and prayed for understanding, she was watching.

And for some reason she had chosen us to be the parents of Melanie.

*She chose us.*

As we tried to grasp this improbable narrative, Katie arrived to tell us it was all true. She had intended to keep Melanie for her first Christmas, she said, and then place her for adoption in the new year. But then she had heard we would be gone for Christmas. And then she thought that maybe it would be best for Melanie to spend her first Christmas with her new parents.

*Her new parents.*

That was us.

Katie wept.

Softly, she told us about eight-week-old Melanie, and what she liked to eat, and when she slept, and some of the special things about her. She offered her crib, and her clothes. She offered everything she had to give.

---

Now she had a question, but the tears were coming in a torrent, choking her words.

She wiped a river from her cheek and took a breath.

Do you like Melanie? she asked.

Do I like Melanie? *Do I like Melanie?* Where would I possibly begin to answer such a question? I had mentally cataloged a profusion of prepared statements about discipline and parenting and hobbies and college funds and a wide assortment of other questions that never came.

*Do I Like Melanie?* I was not prepared for.

I sat quietly, hopelessly searching for a way to craft an answer that would do justice to the question, because I was completely smitten with this baby, and the word *like* was far too dim a descriptor. She asked a second time, perhaps thinking we had not heard.

And then, the meaning of her question finally registered in my mind, as she pulled back a strand of blond hair and rephrased.

Does she look like a Melanie?

And I realized, finally, it was the name.

She just wanted to know if we liked her name.

Pole-axed by emotion, I fumbled to respond, words clotting in my throat. Nothing came out. But as I sat stricken, Stacey lifted her head and smiled to Katie and answered, her voice full of conviction.

Yes, she is a Melanie.

She is a Melanie.

She is most definitely a Melanie.

# Chapter 35

## *The Midnight Run*

You don't even know how you've made my dreams come true, Stacey said to Katie.

Melanie was still sleeping and didn't know her life had just changed forever.

You can take her home now if you like, said Katie.

Somehow a strand of lucidity worked its way back into my brain and I helped everybody decide we should not take actual delivery until we had some papers signed. There were those tales floating around about agreements being rescinded and videos of screaming children yanked away from adoptive parents three years down the road because somebody had forgotten to get something notarized. I wasn't going to allow for that possibility. We made arrangements to sign papers in the morning and pick up Melanie around lunchtime.

The things that go through your head on the way home right after somebody gives you a baby.

Mom is never going to believe we didn't steal this baby, I said.

And your dad is going to have to turn off the air conditioner, Stacey replied.

Right, the air conditioner.

---

My dad grew up in an old farmhouse and was acclimated to sleeping in subarctic temperatures. Things were comfortable enough during waking hours, but at bedtime he would crank the unit down and run it all night, even in the dead of winter. Every Christmas we went home to Tennessee to stay with my parents and Stacey would wake up with blue fingers and blue lips. She was only marginally enthralled, to begin with, by the phenomenon of seeing her breath indoors, but now she would have someone else's warmth to care for.

The next morning I left early to have the adoption paperwork prepared and delivered, every minute thinking this was a powerful but cruel dream. Stacey went to work like always, but in a daze.

I think I might need to leave early, she said to her boss. I'm supposed to be getting a baby today.

She had avoided mentioning to him, until this moment, that she was even contemplating parenthood. He didn't quite know what to say.

The papers were brought back to me with signatures and seals, and I stared at them for a good long while, finally becoming convinced this was happening. I called Stacey.

Your baby is ready, I said.

Are you sure? she asked, breathlessly.

Yes, I said.

She was almost out of the parking lot when her colleague Randy waved down the Beretta.

Do you have a car seat? he asked.

Umm, no.

Of all the things Stacey had purchased in anticipation of this moment that seemed so unlikely, an infant seat wasn't among them.

You can have mine, Randy said. We have an extra.

These are the issues when you receive a baby out of the blue. You aren't prepared for the miracle you prayed for.

---

THE STUCCO HOUSE looked bright now that I was seeing it in the sunshine. Almost like a magical little hand-painted cottage.

It was the simplest of transactions. Melanie was in Karen's arms. A little bag was at her feet, with diapers and two bottles. Here you go, said Karen. Melanie looked into Stacey's face as she was handed over, and then she promptly nestled down into her neck and fell asleep.

Like she belonged there.

---

I WAITED until early evening to call my mom. We toyed with the idea of not telling her anything until we stepped off the plane in Tennessee with Melanie, but decided it would be too much of a shock.

We're going to be bringing some extra luggage, I said when she answered the phone.

We'll pick you up in Dad's car, she replied. It has a big trunk.

What we're bringing can't go in the trunk, I said. We're bringing our new baby.

There was a long silence.

We didn't steal it, I said.

Still, silence.

I recounted the tale, but it was a lot to absorb, starting as I was from scratch. I realized it sounded far-fetched. I didn't know if she was buying the story because she was crying now, and I thought the tears might be because she assumed I would be going to jail.

Later, Mom phoned back a few times to clarify details. By the third call, she was starting to believe.

I've told your dad we're turning up the thermostat when you get here, she said, already anticipating. He can get used to it.

―――

ON OUR SECOND NIGHT—EARLY morning actually—with Melanie, her pacifier had disappeared, as pacifiers are wont to do.

A week before if I had been asked to go to the store before sunup it would have triggered a foul response. Now it seemed a privilege.

There was nobody else shopping in Walgreens when I arrived, only an uninterested little woman behind the counter in her blue vest who looked like she just wanted to get through the night without having a Smith & Wesson shoved in her face.

Where are your pacifiers? I asked, not yet willing to use the term nuk-nuk in public.

She pointed a finger lazily toward a back wall and a moment later I was standing before an exhibition of products more varied than I would ever have imagined.

This would involve a decision. There were pacifiers of blue and green and red and pink. Some translucent. Some with little handles or cartoon characters or elaborate designs.

What would Melanie want? I thought.

I picked up a Gerber three pack with assorted colors that seemed functional. A bit plain, though, so I also grabbed one with an array of little blue stars. Still not quite content in my selections, I took just one more also, featuring Mickey Mouse. I didn't even know Disney was in this business. The Minnie Mouse version, though, looked like something she might like, and she was a girl after all, so I got that one too, just to be safe. And Pluto. And then on the next row there was a colorful one with Elmo, so I took that too. When I removed Elmo from the rack I saw Cookie Monster was hiding just behind, and it didn't feel right to leave him, especially since he was my favorite Sesame Street character and might turn out to be Melanie's favorite too. The pink bib, also, was just too cute to pass by. Plus, a little teether that looked like a baby giraffe.

I lurched to the counter, arms full. The clerk eyed me suspiciously now, undecided whether I was the purchasing agent for a maternity ward or some sort of deviant.

I just got a new baby, I said.

A single eyebrow went up warily as she started scanning.

I mean, we just adopted a baby, I explained.

Just one? she asked. By now she was scanning the eighth pacifier, and admittedly it all seemed dubious.

Her name's Melanie, I said. I want to be sure I have one she likes.

She loaded my items into two plastic bags. It must be a real pain, she said, coming out this time of night for this. Nothing worse than a screaming baby when you just want to get some sleep.

I didn't respond for a bit, trying to grasp how this could ever be a pain, taking care of your baby. Becoming an instant father, just like that. I was the luckiest person in the universe. There's nothing I wouldn't have been willing to do to bring about what had just happened in my life, and yet it had all happened without me doing anything or even knowing what was going on. Awakening to the sound of a crying baby, it was positively symphonic. Rolling out of bed to drive a few miles to get a pacifier for my daughter, it was nothing. I was glad to do it. I mean, genuinely, I was glad to do it. A pain? I was near euphoric, honestly.

I thought about conveying all this to the little woman in Walgreens, in the middle of the night, but I knew it wouldn't come out right.

So I just grabbed my bags and I smiled and I tipped my ball cap, and I said—

You know, the truth is, I don't mind it. I don't mind it at all.

---

IT WAS STILL dark as I turned north for home. There was a welcome chill in the air, and I lowered the car windows. My route took me along an avenue that rises above the city and coils through the hills of Thunderbird Park. The streetlamps dropped behind me and the air cooled some more. I was in the desert peaks, enveloped in an inky blackness. In my mirror, a sea of lights and millions of people slumbered, lifeless and oblivious of my mission. The city withdrew and receded behind a ridge, and the stars brightened, illuminating the heavens and blinking their joy.

Coming back down the hill now, and a humble little scattering of lights began to assemble in the distance. Somewhere in that brightening cluster, I knew, was my wife and my baby, waiting for me and my delivery.

*My wife and my baby!* I said it out loud to myself, as if to be sure.

Beyond, there was the slightest hue on the horizon. Just the deepest blue, nothing more, but the preliminary promise the sun would be on its way, as surely as the day before, but different now and forevermore.

    I don't mind this, I said again, this time louder and laughing, and only to myself, and to God, and as I heard the sound of my own voice, I knew it wasn't a dream.

    I don't mind this at all.

# Chapter 36

## *The Inheritance*

Daddy, can we go swing? Melanie asked.

Yes, we can, Sweet Pea.

Five blocks up and one block over from our house was an elementary school with a nice playground and big new swings. We were trespassing, according to the sign, but no one ever said anything.

Here on the swing, her glee was extracted in spades. The blond hair flapping, the head thrust back joyfully, baring the little white scar on the chin where she slipped on the patio. The cascading laughter, the little feet carving expertly through the air. And absolutely no fear.

Higher, Daddy, higher! she demanded, from way above.

Back home there was another one now, a second miracle gift, a son. I knew a couple of years would pass in a flash, and Taylor would soon be here too, demanding his own private carnival sessions.

What will I be able to give them? I wondered. When the swing becomes a fledgling childhood memory. We were never going to be millionaires from the looks of it and, in truth, were still just getting by. And then I remembered the secret fund.

---

My dad has a bit of money. I want it when he goes. Not for me. For the children. I don't want ESJ to get her hands on it, that's true enough, but the motivation isn't greed. Really, it's not.

A huge sum it most assuredly is not. There would be more if he'd decided on some other line of work, but when you devote yourself to saving souls you don't build up large inheritances for others to enjoy. Pay is mediocre, subject to reduction without notice. Retirement plan a joke. You travel the world, but its steerage class all the way.

Never had a problem with it growing up, but now that I'm thinking about an inheritance, it seems like Dad didn't really think it through, this idea of casting off for parts unknown, leaving almost everyone you love behind.

---

I saw it, the first time, when I wasn't even tall enough to reach the drawer. In their bedroom, where I wasn't supposed to be without asking. But we had wood floors instead of carpet on account of my asthma, and you heard anyone coming down the hall from a mile off. Built-in warning system. So I muscled a chair over, hopped up and slid it open.

I don't know what you would call it officially. I called it the tie tack drawer.

Dad had a lot of tie tacks to go with his handsome tie collection. He had gold and silver and pewter, some with monograms, a few embedded with precious stones, or pretending to be. Some shaped like states, or crosses. My favorite was the gold kangaroo tie tack—he had a bunch of those. He bought the kangaroos at some Brisbane jeweler to give as gifts when back in America, and there were always four or five of them in the tie tack drawer.

And also, a couple of old watches, a bunch of cuff links and some silk handkerchiefs.

And in the back corner, a little brown envelope. It was a bit crumpled on the edges and had been sealed at one point, but the years had dried up and cracked the adhesive. And it had writing on it. Too bad I wasn't old enough to read, because I couldn't very well go ask Dad what the words said on the envelope in the drawer in his room I wasn't supposed to be in. Inside the envelope, three shiny silver dollars.

I loved rifling through the tie tack drawer whenever I had the opportunity, loved the little clinking noise the trinkets made when I stirred them around, loved to pick up the cuff links and feel their weightiness in my palm. But always, in the back corner, that little envelope. A little tilt of the hand, and those silver dollars would slide out smartly. I would think about what I could buy with those coins. American money was no good in Australia, but I imagined their value as immeasurable—certainly enough to get everything I ever wanted. Why they would be just sitting here, unused and useless, I couldn't fathom. And then, gingerly, I would slide them back in their weathered packet and replace it with careful precision back in its assigned place in the drawer.

When I started school I could read what was on the envelope, but I didn't understand what it meant. The words were in Dad's handwriting and they said—

*To Be Spent When God Stops Providing.*

What could it mean? I wondered. For years, I wondered.

It was a decade later, perhaps, and we were moving again,

loading up the barrels. Among my duties was the packing of the tie tack drawer. Finally, an opportunity to ask the meaning of the words on the envelope, the reason for the three silver dollars.

There was this lady, my dad said, I don't remember her name anymore. I was seventeen and leaving home to study for the ministry. She came up to me in church and gave me the silver dollars. Gave them to me in this very envelope.

It was a nice gift, from a woman who probably didn't have much money to a farm kid who definitely didn't.

I took them to college with me, Dad continued, and I wrote these words on the envelope. If I ever got to the point of really needing this money, I would know God had let me down and I could go back to the farm. That was a long time ago.

So far, so good.

He stood there for a moment, wistful.

He handed the envelope back to me. Don't lose these, he said.

*To Be Spent When God Stops Providing.* Sixty years it's been since he wrote that. Millions of miles. Joy and heartache. Surprises and tragedies. Tie tacks have come and gone and come and gone again. Watches stopped their ticking. Cufflinks, who knows where.

The envelope remains.

———

MELANIE IS ten feet in the air now, at the top of a graceful arc with her face and body parallel to the ground, which is layered with hard mulch. The giggles pouring out are absolutely delicious. A little ripple of terror runs through me. What would happen if her hands slipped from the swing about now, or if she just let go? Kids, they don't appreciate the laws of physics. I am performing some rudimentary geometry in my head so that if she falls, from any point, I will intercept her before she faceplants into the mulch.

She doesn't know it, but me being here, ready to make the catch, is just a temporary thing. The thought of it makes me just a little sad. But one day when I'm gone, she'll have the inheritance.

# Chapter 37

## *The First Rule*

Jim Craney holds up a finger and points it at you, sort of.

First rule, he says. Pay attention.

The finger is crooked now and arthritic and he shakes so much the aim isn't true. Near a miracle, though, that digit is still attached, along with the other nine.

You will not forget the first rule. He doesn't allow it. God forbid it's your turn to play a card and your mind has wandered off for a moment. Or worse, the traffic light turns green and you fail to punch the gas within a nanosecond.

Jim Craney learned to pay attention as foreman at the A-1 Cabinet Shop, Inc., located on the blue-collar end of West Osborn Road in Phoenix. Any time and every time some inebriated or hungover chump ran a hand through a sawblade or sliced an artery, or took a high velocity splinter in the cornea, it was Jim Craney who took them to the hospital. They would be bleeding—and many times screaming—and Jim would mutter to himself,

I tried to tell him and he didn't listen, first rule.

He generally kept these horror stories to himself but every so often they filtered into the conversation at dinner, and the three little kids would sit there at the table wide-eyed and terrified. Jim would sense the fear he had stirred up and reassure them he was safe, and everybody would be OK as long as they remembered. And he would point the finger and say it again.

First rule, pay attention. I pay attention, always.

Stacey would look at her dad's hands. They were not withered then, but handsome and strong and steady and superhuman. Still, she worried.

Every morning it was the same thing. The alarm clock buzzed for one person but stirred two. Jim Craney would roll out of bed and begin his four thirty in the morning routine. Across the hall Stacey would start praying that her dad would come back with all his fingers.

You provide, but you don't make a lot of money working at a cabinet shop. You live in a house that's adequate. You have a swamp cooler instead of an air conditioner. Your floor is linoleum, the kind that carries sound all over the house.

———

It was that linoleum, inevitably, that carried the sound of Stacey's dad as he trudged through the blackness into the kitchen. She knew every sound by heart. The ratcheting opening of a can of Campbell's. The unscrewing of the thermos lid, the pouring of the soup, and again the cap, twisting back on. The sharp, tinny snap of his lunch box opening, the rustle of saltines going in the box, the lid clasping shut.

There was the click as the door was unlocked, though she didn't actually hear it open, because all the hinges were well-oiled. The muffled closing of the door, and off he went to the giant spinning blades and knives and chisels, and the idiots wielding them who didn't pay attention.

And every day, Jim Crancy came back home with the ten fingers. And he brought back the cabinet tacks.

The tacks, those were the things.

He was a slight man. She didn't think it then but realizes now. Yet sinewy and strong and he had a thunderous pair of steel-toed boots. He would arrive home smelling of sawdust and varnish and sweat, grab the *Arizona Republic,* and hoist the feet on the ottoman and the kids would pull the tacks out of the bottom of his shoes while he read the paper.

Evidently there were a lot of cabinet tacks laying around the floor at the A-1 Cabinet Shop. Never did a workday end without a dozen or more of them embedded in those thick soles. There was something cathartic and eminently gratifying about it, pulling the tacks out of daddy's shoes. At first it would be impossible, your little fingers struggling for a hold. And then with time and effort you could work your nail under the head and jiggle it back and forth a little to get it loose. Then you would wedge a couple of small fingers under and pull in earnest until it loosened and surrendered, sliding out smoothly.

With all the tacks removed he would lie down on the floor and put the paper over his head and take a quick nap. Until the doorbell rang. The neighborhood kids, from every which way, asking.

Can your dad come out and play?

Sure he can.

Whatever they played, he played, and dominated. Baseball, football, bike racing, kickball, anything you want. Pay attention and watch this.

And down the road a few years, there were the cars. Not expensive, but fast. Jim could supercharge anything, and he supercharged his cars to win. He purchased one new car in his life, a 1968 Dodge Dart four door, sticker price $2,297, base model. It did not remain a base model after purchase. A law-abiding man he was, always, except in the car. Speed limits were for the great derisible, ponderous masses who didn't pay attention.

The Dart was unimposing to look upon, but you didn't have any way of knowing what he had done under the hood, and his reflexes were lightning and he would be away before your brain had registered the traffic signal had changed.

Stacey's driving lessons were unique. Started with the inevitable first rule, pay attention.

Second rule, drive with both feet. Left foot for the brake, right foot for the gas. You can't afford the fraction of a second it takes to move your foot from one pedal to the other. That's wasted time.

The right lane is for losers. Get in the fast lane and go.

Don't get passed by anyone.

Take that corner like you mean it. This isn't a cruise ship.

Don't ever get beat off the line. Ever.

Watch the other drivers. Not just the car in front of you, but the one in front of that. Watch where they're looking, their head, their body language. They're not paying attention.

By the time Stacey was in high school the Dodge Dart was a relic. Finely tuned and fast, still, but a relic. She would feel the crimson surge across her face as she was dropped off and picked up for school. The other rich kids with their Camaros and Porsches, and then her dad pulling up with the fine coating of sawdust and the tan Dodge. Not cool.

Long time ago, that was. Stacey is telling her dad how she's embarrassed now by the embarrassment she felt then.

That's OK, Jim said, and he laughed, with a touch of reticence. He always comes across a little sheepish when the stories are recounted.

He is still slight in stature but not in character, though the decades of hard manual labor have come to fetch their due. The wrinkles are etched deep and there's a shuffle in his step and stiffness to his back, and the A-1 Cabinet Shop has long since ceased to exist. He's telling the tales he withheld when she was little.

There was more menacing him than just the iron teeth of the saw blades. He's talking about the guys who wanted to take him out, every now and then. Kill the foreman. The Shop didn't draw the upper echelon of the workforce, and it was not a background check kind of a place. People had to be fired sometimes. And when they were fired, they were fired by Jim Craney, and they were not infrequently somebody's brother or cousin who was just out of the pen, or in a gang, or somebody who knew people.

Outside the Shop, Jim would face them up. They were always bigger than him.

Word is you want to take me out, he would say. Now's the time. Take your best shot.

They would look him over, radiating hate. Then the eyes would drop, and they would walk away.

This happened, it turns out, more than a time or two.

How did you know they weren't packing? Stacey asked.

First rule, he said.

He is dealing the cards with his wobbly hand and trash talking like he wins most of the time, which he doesn't. Which only makes the trash talking funnier. He conjures up riotous monikers on the fly and they come out of his mouth before he's contemplated whether they are going to be remotely intelligible. The kids and the grandkids are gathered around to hear what nonsensical insult will come flying next and the entertainment value is tremendous.

Somewhere in between all this Stacey brings up the memory of the tacks.

Those cabinet tacks, she said. We loved to pull those out of your boots. I lived for that, every day.

There's a pause. He's contemplating a response, and the room falls quiet. Whatever will he say next? Whatever, it will be good.

Those tacks, he said. I guess I can tell you now.

He has the sheepish look again.

The first time I came home with a couple tacks in my boots, he said, I saw how much you loved pulling them out.

Truth is, he continued, we kept the floor pretty clean at A-1. So every day, just before leaving, I sat down and pushed the tacks into my soles. For you.

Every day? Stacey asked.

Yes, Jim Craney said. Every day.

It's Stacey's turn but she can't play. She can't see her cards because her eyes are filled with tears.

Jim Craney gives her a minute, and after the crying there is laughing and then he points at the deck in her hand and he says —softly this time—we're waiting, it's your turn, first rule.

# Chapter 38

## *The Derby*

There's nothing like the feeling of being omnipotent, infallible, unstoppable, unbeatable. It's one of the more attractive features of being the father of a seven-year-old boy. Enjoying hero status by default, without doing much of anything. You can be a total buffoon and still have adoration heaped on you by an innocent child.

This wouldn't last, I certainly knew that. But I was in no rush to disabuse Taylor of his worshipful notions. Might as well ride it for as long as possible, I was thinking.

The upcoming derby presented a serious threat to that plan.

I thought churches were supposed to help you strengthen your family, but I felt this one was trying to undermine me with their annual miniature pinewood derby for the kids. The idea, I suppose, was to create a bonding experience wherein father and son would work together to craft a beautiful and brisk racecar. A couple of weeks before the derby, the church supplied a kit containing a crude block of wood, cheap plastic wheels and toothpick axles. The rest was going to be up to me.

It's a decent idea if your father has any skills. But for someone like me there was no upside, only the singular prospect of having my aura of invincibility destroyed.

———

My deficiencies in woodworking—not to mention metalworking, auto mechanics, absolutely anything involving electricity, and any of the other industrial arts—were well chronicled and in some regions had reached legendary status. I had a vast hoard of building blocks as a child that may have suggested I might be predisposed to the construction trade, but as time went by it became clear that Legos were at the upper limit of my capabilities. I did not make any inquiry into joining the Boy Scouts, fearful they would have rejected my membership request outright or otherwise expel me as soon as they saw me in action.

I did make efforts when required. In England, Kingswood school required every male student to take woodworking. I built a bookshelf that not only could not support books, it could not support its own weight. It collapsed immediately. The instructor Mr. Fitch, his face pinched in anguish at the sight of it, recommended that I throw away the pieces and just watch the other boys and learn from them.

On the next project—I don't remember what it was, but it doesn't matter—my chisel became stuck in a piece of wood just as Mr. Fitch arrived, hovering over my shoulder to observe. I nervously tugged at the imbedded tool with increasing force and mounting embarrassment. Mr. Fitch—and now others who had stopped their own work to take in the spectacle—looked on with something like disbelief. I pulled at the thing desperately until it suddenly came loose, but with both hands and my whole body invested in freeing the chisel, my thrust propelled the handle swiftly back into my own cheek.

This demonstration of the law of momentum was not complete, however, as I stumbled backward, caught my ankle on the edge of a sawhorse leg and disappeared gracefully into a pile of scrap wood. Mr. Fitch was of no help in the matter, doubled over as he was for the next five minutes, and wiping tears from his eyes. After many failed efforts to collect himself, he eventually croaked out an order sending me off to the school nurse for treatment to the gash below my eye.

The school's most egregious blunder was giving me access to fire. For some reason, they felt it would be useful for schoolboys to learn how to make pottery. I was relatively harmless when making a clay bowl, if you will make allowances for the fact that it was never close to being spherical. The real trouble came during the glazing process.

Fiddling with the controls on the blowtorch one afternoon, I had trouble adjusting the dial which regulated the fuel flow. Agitated, I became fixated on the device itself rather than the direction my nozzle was pointing. I failed to notice it was angled towards the head of a nearby student, who was preoccupied with his own assignment. In a single unfortunate moment, I rotated the dial from *idle* to *erupt* and a gigantic flame shot out, enveloping the young man's head. He fell to the floor with a hellish scream, and after the initial panic abated his mates inventoried his face and observed him to be short an eyebrow and very ruddy-complected. Whispers of smoke drifted up from what was left of his collar.

Then they turned toward me, far from satisfied with my fumbling avowals of apology. The teacher arrived just as I was about to have my face kicked in, but the experience nevertheless was a stern reminder that I did not have the skills for honest blue-collar work.

WITH THIS BACKGROUND, I did everything possible to beg off the pinewood derby. Taylor knew nothing of my deficits and was expecting me to carve out and design a racecar that would be lightning fast. He fully believed he would win and never even considered the possibility of defeat, since Dad was involved in the project. I, on the other hand, knew anything I designed would not only come last, but would further be an object of ridicule.

I staved off the inevitable for a couple of years. Taylor came home with his bag of parts at age five which he gave me for safekeeping and, somehow, it got lost while under my stewardship. On the night of the race, I distracted him with a Happy Meal and the suggestion we peruse the toy aisles at Target. It was enough to sweep all thoughts of the grand prix from his mind, and I was off the hook.

At age six, I told him we couldn't go because we had family plans.

What plans? he asked. I want you to build my race car. I want to win the grand prix.

Well, umm, we can't. We're going to a movie, all of us, together, I said. We're going to have a fantastic family night. It'll be way more fun than the grand prix. Also I will buy you some more toys.

There was some mild resistance, but ultimately he succumbed.

The third year there was no avoiding it any longer. I tried the normal diversionary tactics along with some new ones, all without success. He was consumed with the grand prix, having seen the trophies to be awarded and having listened to other kids boast about the cars they were building with their fathers. And then to make matters worse, my wife piled on.

You need to do this for him, she said.

You have no idea how bad this is going to be, I replied with a touch of scorn.

That's silly—it will great, said Stacey, in the same tone of voice she used when encouraging preschoolers to go potty. I stormed out. She was obviously choosing to misremember some of the carpentry projects I had worked on around the house in years past, including the one where I fell through the ceiling.

With great trepidation, I took the block of wood out to the garage. I hacked at it for several evenings, eventually carving rudimentary depressions in each end that could pass for a hood and trunk, as long as someone was there to offer the interpretation. I then gouged out a hole in the undercarriage and glued in some tiny weights that had been provided in the kit. Taylor helped by painting it blue and adding some stickers. It was truly ridiculous.

Saturday morning of the event, I tried to temper expectations on the drive over to church.

You know, Taylor, I said, there are probably going to be a lot of people at the grand prix. We might not win, but we'll just try to have fun anyway, no matter what happens.

My car's going to win, he replied. I know it will, because you built it.

My heart hurt for the disappointment about to cloud his world.

We walked into the fellowship hall. I looked around and swallowed hard. It was worse than I imagined. This was like a real race, with judges and serious competitors and spectators and—most intimidating of all—the fathers. Several of them were bona-fide engineers in real life and were lugging around small toolboxes with sophisticated equipment for last minute adjustments. They had little mini-sanders and polishers and drills and gauges and files and suspicious lubricants which, frankly, I do not believe could be purchased at the Home Depot.

My accessories consisted of some scotch tape and extra weights to tape to the bottom of the car.

We were motioned to a table where the cars were all laid out for pre-race inspection, and here I had to beat down an overpowering urge to flee. Most of the other entries were absolutely magnificent. Brilliantly sculptured, painted exquisitely and fine-tuned beyond anything I had ever contemplated. Several were dead ringers for Indy cars. NASCAR was also well represented with numerous immaculate replicas, and there were imaginative recreations of everything from a '57 Chevy to the Scooby van. One father had fashioned a banana split car so realistic it looked ready to eat.

I overheard two of the fathers discussing the intricacies of the test tracks they had constructed in their homes. One had converted a spare bedroom while the other had used his garage, and they were debating how much the variances in humidity would have affected the testing sessions. It occurred to me, at this late moment, that I had not even checked to see if our car would roll.

Taylor placed his pathetic car proudly on the table and we checked in. The almost palpable stare of many sets of incredulous eyeballs—rotating from the Taylormobile to Taylor to me and then back again, thankfully seemed to be beyond the awareness of my son.

And then, the critiques started rolling in from his peers.

Your car is ugly, one little girl said.

Asked another: Is it supposed to be a bus?

It doesn't have any windows, someone else observed.

And then this helpful query from a sympathetic boy: Why didn't you ask your dad to help you?

Taylor was unfazed, and as the judges began inspecting the

entries and making notations on their clipboards, he didn't seem bothered that scant attention was paid to his car. They were, after all, looking for winners in the categories of Workmanship, Originality and Appearance, and he didn't care about that. His singular interest was the Speed trophy.

---

It was time for the first heat—which would surely be our only heat—and I was working out in my head how I would manage the letdown, the sense of betrayal, the loss of wonder about to be foisted upon my son. His brick of a car was placed on the track with three others. A choir of chuckles rippled across the room. In a few moments it would all be over. The referee lifted the gate, and off they went down the slope.

Taylor's car started grudgingly—I was happy it was moving at all—and immediately settled into last place. Even the banana split, built purely for show, was ahead of the Taylormobile. I stole a quick glance at my son who was beyond excited but who, in my mind, was Vinko Bogataj barreling down the ski ramp on *Wide World of Sports* about to suffer the agony of defeat.

Halfway down the slope, I bemusedly saw Taylor's racer was suddenly and unexpectedly surging forward, as if propelled by an unseen magical force. As the three competitors reached the bottom of the track and began to peter out, the Taylormobile was still gathering momentum. In a wink it rocketed past the others and shot to the finish line, two feet clear.

Stunning. By some twist of fate, Taylor had evidently been drawn against the weakest participants in the field. We weren't slowest after all. Disappointment was merely deferred until round two, but this was an unexpected blessing to have won a heat. I could spin that a little bit and not look like a total failure.

And then I noticed a few of the dads conferring among themselves, their faces draped with worry. They had been at this enough to know a fast car when they saw one. I began to recognize—from the gestures, the pallid expressions, the muffled conversations and most of all the anxious inquiries they were now fielding from their own children—that something considered impossible was unfolding. The Taylormobile, somehow, was a competitor.

Heat Two. Now the Taylormobile was drawn against other winners, and I tamped down my hopes. But the result was the same. The ugly little block started last but exploded down the track and thundered past the other hapless rivals, whose owners were truly stricken by the scene.

We were now one heat away from the final, and a wave of alarm was sweeping through the room. Competitors who had been eliminated from the competition encircled me, asking for secrets to be revealed.

I replied with a shrug of the shoulders. I wasn't sandbagging. There was nothing to tell.

By some sheer, mad coincidence, or the intervention of a benevolent and mischievous God, I had accidently built a rocket ship. The odds against it were absurdly infinitesimal.

Semifinal—not even close. At this point my son was beginning to taunt the losers. I had to restrain him and familiarize him with the concept of graciousness.

The final pitted the Taylormobile against cars designed by a software developer and two engineers—gentlemen who happened to know me and my acute limitations. They understood, unhappily, that they and their children were about to become victims of one of the greatest flukes in the history of physical science. It wasn't a runaway, but not a photo finish either. The Taylormobile barreled across the line in first place and into victory lane.

Congratulations were offered, mostly through gritted teeth and forced smiles, and at various corners of the room words of consolation were shared with those in tears. The trophy presentation ceremony was laden with an aura of disappointment, shock and bitterness.

Except for the beaming face of Taylor, oblivious to all the suffering. He was the one person in the room who wasn't surprised. It was exactly what he had expected.

On the drive home, he never let go of the trophy or the smile.

---

STACEY and I walked into the kitchen. She began assembling a pot of chili. I sat down at the table, dumbfounded. How did that happen? I asked.

Before she could answer, Taylor entered, the trophy hoisted triumphantly above his head. $1^{st}$ *Place*, it said, in big golden letters, and on the bottom was the word *Speed*, in even larger golden letters. His face was still broadcasting at about a thousand kilowatts.

I don't really know how to explain this, I said. You know I had no clue what I was doing.

Stacey laughed. Yes, she replied, but it doesn't matter now.

I mean, look at this thing, I said.

I took the Taylormobile and set it on the kitchen table. One of the wheels had fallen off already. Lost in the post-race celebration, but further proof of my ineptitude.

I rolled it along the table with my finger, the little three-wheeled miracle.

I would never have dreamed we had a chance, I said. That place was teeming with experts. And they were none too happy with the way this thing played out.

Well, the experts, they don't always know everything, said Stacey.

Taylor had left the kitchen and now was looping the living room, searching for the perfect spot to display his trophy, now clasped tightly in the crook of his arm.

This is more than I deserved, I said.

Yeah, Stacey laughed. Who would have believed it?

CPSIA information can be obtained
at www.ICGtesting.com
Printed in the USA
BVHW021816131222
654137BV00019B/175/J